DATE DUE

I Saw Mommy Kicking Santa Claus

The ultimate holiday survival guide

A PERIGEE BOOK

I Saw Mommy Kicking Santa Claus

The ultimate holiday survival guide

Ann Hodgman

PERIGEE BOOKS
Published by the Penguin Group
Penguin Group (USA) Inc.
375 Hudson Street, New York, New York 10014, U.S.A.
Penguin Group (Canada), 10 Alcorn Avenue, Toronto, Ontario, Canada M4V 3B2
(a division of Pearson Penguin Canada Inc.)
Penguin Books Ltd., 80 Strand, London WC2R 0RL, England
Penguin Group Ireland, 25 St. Stephen's Green, Dublin 2, Ireland (a division of Penguin Books, Ltd.)
Penguin Group (Australia), 250 Camberwell Road, Camberwell, Victoria 3124, Australia
(a division of Pearson Australia Group Pty., Ltd.)
Penguin Books India Pvt. Ltd., 11 Community Centre, Panchsheel Park, New Delhi—110 017, India
Penguin Group (NZ), Cnr. Airborne and Rosedale Roads, Albany, Auckland, New Zealand
(a division of Pearson New Zealand, Ltd.)
Penguin Books (South Africa) (Pty.) Ltd., 24 Sturdee Avenue, Rosebank, Johannesburg 2196, South Africa

Penguin Books Ltd., Registered Offices: 80 Strand, London, WC2R 0RL, England

This book is an original publication of Perigee Books.

Excerpt from *The International Family: Simple Rituals to Strengthen Family Ties*, copyright © 1997, by William J. Doherty, Ph.D. Reprinted by permission of the author.

Copyright © 2004 by Ann Hodgman
Cover design by Charles Björklund
Cover and interior art by Victoria Roberts
Text design by Tiffany Estreicher

First edition: November 2004

Perigee hardcover ISBN: 0-399-53042-8

Library of Congress Cataloging-in-Publication Data

Hodgman, Ann.
  I saw mommy kicking Santa Claus : the ultimate holiday survival guide / Ann Hodgman.
    p. cm.
    ISBN 0-399-53042-8
    1. Christmas—Psychological aspects. 2. Stress (Psychology). 3. Depression, Mental. I. Title.

GT4985.H543 2004
394.2663—dc22   2004053361

PRINTED IN THE UNITED STATES OF AMERICA

10 9 8 7 6 5 4 3 2 1

Lorf to Cootie. Lolo. and Nood from Oon

Every year at Christmastime a whole set of emotions sweeps
over me—emotions which probably go back to my childhood.
The first emotion is wondering if I'm going to get any presents.
Then it changes to "Hooray, I got some presents!" Then it
changes to "Is that all the presents I got?"

—JACK HANDY, FUZZY MEMORIES

Contents

Introduction

What Do You Really Want for Christmas?

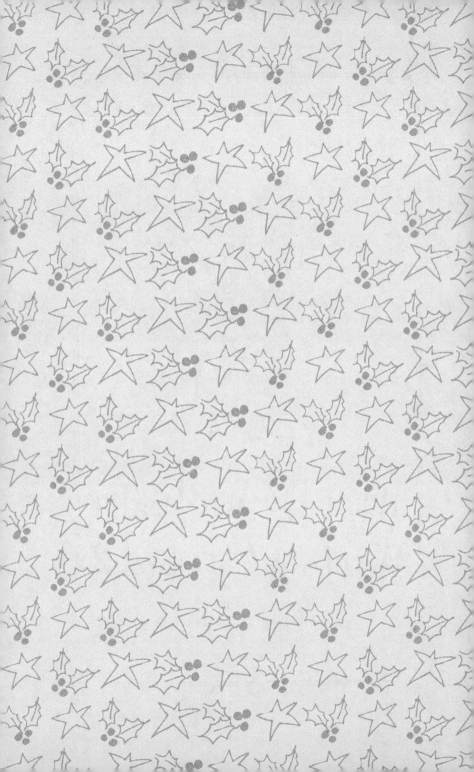

> "Christmas had become something to endure at least as much as it had become something to enjoy—something to dread at least as much as something to look forward to."
>
> —BILL MCKIBBEN, *HUNDRED DOLLAR HOLIDAY*

Close your eyes. No, wait, open them back up. You're going to need to be able to read this.

Now I want you to ask yourself this question: What would be the perfect Christmas for you?

The first image that pops into my head when I ask *myself* this question is impossibly hokey, but whaddaya gonna do? If I can't tell you about it, we'll never get off on the right foot. It's a vision of me being pulled along in the Budweiser sleigh. But isn't that everyone's image of a perfect Christmas?

My other imagined "perfect" Christmas is set on a cold, starry night. I'm driving along (in my car, not a sleigh) on a quiet country road when I pass a house that's beautifully decorated for Christmas. Its windows are all lit up, and golden light is streaming out the front door, which is being opened for some guests who have just arrived. They're rushing up to the

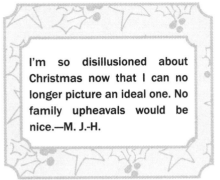

I'm so disillusioned about Christmas now that I can no longer picture an ideal one. No family upheavals would be nice.—M. J.-H.

door, and the people inside the house are rushing out to greet them. I love watching them, but rather than join in the festivities I just speed on by in the dark.

What does this image mean? I'm not sure, but it's got some elements that are worth noticing.

First: This idyllic vision is not a bit like the way I actually celebrate Christmas. My typical holiday is more likely to include clenched teeth and cries of "Stop taking the Scotch tape!" than familial bliss. If this vision is truly my ideal Christmas, I'd better try to incorporate *something* like it *somewhere* into my holidays.

Second: I'm feeling peacefully alone in the fantasy. Even though I enjoy watching the big celebration from afar, I also cherish my autonomy in this vision. Of course, the traditional Christmas is rarely spent in a nice quiet car—so again, if this image spells perfection to me, I'd better at least set aside some time I can be by myself.

Third, and perhaps iffiest and most speculative (but again, I think it's worth paying attention to): It seems that, for me, Christmas may be more about the process of traveling somewhere than actually arriving there.

Fourth: The house I drive by is that lit-up mansion from those old Chivas Regal magazine ads. I seem to be more strongly influenced by alcohol advertising than I had realized.

I don't know what your perfect Christmas fantasy is. But I bet you're like me in that it's totally different from your real Christmas. If this is true, don't be sad. Not even children get everything they want for Christmas. Besides, who's to say that a fantasy is actually what you want in real life? If my entire

Christmas experience consisted of going for a drive—in either a sleigh or a car—I doubt I'd really jump out at the end and exclaim "Best Christmas ever!" I bet I'd feel as if something were missing.

Still, you shouldn't lose sight of the image that pops into your head as you do this exercise. If you keep turning it over and thinking about what the holiday means to you, you can start to incorporate the most important aspects in your holiday celebration this year. And that's really the key to having a more meaningful Christmas.

Now I'm going to tell you a secret I've never told anyone before, not even my family. *Especially* not my family.

When my kids were little and Christmas was at its most hectic, I used to go to church a total of *three* times in a twenty-four-hour period—twice on Christmas Eve (once to the children's service with the kids, once to the longer midnight mass)—and then again to the chapel service on Christmas morning by myself. The Christmas morning service at my church is beautiful—quiet, peaceful, and austere. Nevertheless, one year it occurred to me as I started to drive up the same road to church for the third service in less than a day: *What I* really *need is some time by myself!* Abruptly, I drove on past the church and headed to the next town.

I spent the following hour just driving around, looking at people's houses. Some were furred with swags, wreaths, and lighting; some were plainer. In one field I saw a horse running happily around by itself. Inside most of the houses, I knew, people were celebrating Christmas in all kinds of ways. Some of the families had children who were still opening their presents. Some were expecting

I would love just one Christmas where my husband had fun. —A. D.

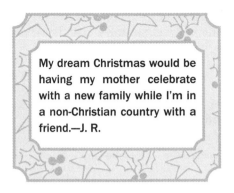

My dream Christmas would be having my mother celebrate with a new family while I'm in a non-Christian country with a friend.—J. R.

company and racing around to get ready. In some, Christmas was already over. But I myself had been temporarily cut loose from the whole process. For a little while, I was free just to be a Christmas observer.

I came home from the drive feeling calm, unrumpled, and more ready for Christmas Day than even the chapel service would have made me feel. It only occurred to me later that the drive had come very close to my image of a perfect Christmas.

For several years thereafter, I would say good-bye to everyone, head off toward my church, and keep driving for an hour. Gradually I learned how to make Christmas less frantic for all of us. Gradually, too, my children started sleeping late enough on Christmas morning that there was no Christmas frenzy for me to escape. Now my son and daughter wake up at around 11:00 A.M. (I'm sorry to torture those of you with small children, but your turn will come.) That gives me a calm enough morning that I no longer need to escape into the car to be by myself.

I realize that in telling this secret, I've forgone the chance to have my peaceful, secret Christmas morning drives if I ever need them again—for example, if I'm spending Christmas in a house with small children, which I assume will happen to me at some point. But I don't care. Now that I've identified the elements of a perfect Christmas for myself, I'll be able to figure out a different way to get a break from all the chaos if I need it.

Maybe I'll take a walk on Christmas night after everyone else is in bed. Maybe on Christmas morning I'll just be brave enough to say, "I'm going for a drive—back in an hour." And if that's the case, I'll let people do what they want about the presents. (After all, people whose first choice it is to take a private drive on Christmas morning can't have everything.) Maybe I'll save my escape until the day after Christmas. Who knows?

One thing I've discovered over the years is that you have to take Christmas where you find it. The Christmas spirit is elusive. It doesn't steadily rain down on everything day after day. If you're an adult, you're lucky to feel Christmas-y *once* during the whole season. But if you know what it is you'd like best for Christmas, you've got a better chance of capturing that moment.

That's what this book will help you do. By figuring out what *you* really want for Christmas—a cozy dinner with family and friends, a festive tree-trimming afternoon, or (like me) a blessedly quiet hour on Christmas Day—you can start planning your next holiday to make it a reality.

1

Are You Flunking Christmas?

Dark is the season, dark our hearts and shut to mystery.
—CAROL CHRISTOPHER DRAKE, "WHAT IS THE CRYING AT JORDAN?"

Before we know it, the holidays will be upon us again. Ugh.

No, wait—that wasn't how I was going to start this. I was going to be way more upbeat. All about how Christmas is over before I've even stopped dreading it, and how every January there's a tinge of melancholy as I begin to put away the Christmas decorations. Especially because *no one* will help me do it. Oh, sure, they like to trim the tree and bake cookies and arrange the creche on the windowsill, but when it comes to taking things off the tree and washing the cookie sheets and trying to figure out how the little creche guys all fit back into the little box . . .

No, wait—I wasn't going to dwell on that. I was going to say something like, "There's a tinge of melancholy, certainly, but the memory of our happy holidays will sustain me through the year ahead." (Although what the hell am I supposed to do with our leftover tree now that I've missed the deadline for the town tree-pickup? Will this be like the Christmas a few years ago, when the tree stayed up until March and almost burst into flames whenever we so much as breathed on it?)

But forget about those details. This is supposed to be a time when my heart is alight with love and anticipation. Every chore is a blessing instead of a burden, because it's helping to celebrate the birth of baby Jesus even more perfectly. (Therefore, whenever I feel cranky or tense, I'm not *just* cranky or tense—I'm also letting down baby Jesus, who's lying there in that manger feeling very disappointed in me.)

Okay, so maybe I need this book about recapturing holiday cheer as much as we all do. If you're anything like me, here are just a few of the issues and questions Christmas stirs up in most people every year:

"I don't have any money!" How much should you spend? How much can you afford to spend? How can you devise a way to spend much, much more than you can afford? How can you conceal the fact that you've spent four times as much as you promised your spouse you'd spend? How can you pay for last Christmas before the heavy foot of *next* Christmas bears down upon you and crushes you into the dirt?

"My children think I don't love them enough!" Obviously you want to use this blessed, blessed time to demonstrate your love for your children. But should you do that by giving them every present they ask for? What if you don't provide everything on the list, and the kids end up disappointed? What if you *do* provide everything on the list—down to the last Barbie shoe— and thereby prove to them that yes, love *is* a question of giving people every material thing they want?

"I have to keep up all the traditions!" Now that you've moved out of your parents' house and started your own Christmases, how many

of your family's customs should you import and install in your own home? How many do you have a right to? How many does your spouse have a right to? Whose family had better traditions? And of course that really means, whose family is better? (Yours.)

"Who's making Christmas special for me?*"* No matter how old you are, and how alive your parents may be, when you're an adult it's hard to shed the feeling that someone else is supposed to be taking care of Christmas for you. It's so unfair! When did you turn into the one who has to make other people happy? Where's the grown-up who's supposed to be making *you* happy? (And don't look at your spouse.)

"I'm going to hell!" If you're a Christian, this holiday is second only to Easter (which still seems less important only because it has fewer shopping days). But that nice holy glow keeps getting buried under piles of wrapping paper and receipts. The closer the countdown brings you to Christmas, the less church-y you feel. By Christmas Eve—the time you've been absolutely counting on church to give you the sanctified Christmas buzz that was going to carry you through the marathon of the next morning—you've been prodded and jabbed into such a state of feverish anxiety that all you can do during the midnight service is pick at your cuticles and check your watch.

What Child Is This?

The absolute worst Christmas we ever had when my son was seven and opened every present under the tree before the rest of us were even downstairs. His, most of ours, our daughter's . . . I was enough of a Christmas-hater to begin with, and this just sent me around the bend.—N. S.

"And on top of it all, what about my presents?*"* I know, I know. We're all adults now. We know that Christmas

All I Want for Christmas...

When my sister and I were little, we opened a box under the tree and found two blankets with horses on them. My sister thought it meant we were getting horses for Christmas and was incredibly excited. It turned out we were getting bunk beds.—D. O.

isn't about what you find under the tree. But, but, but . . . but don't you secretly feel that a pretty big part of Christmas *is* about what you find under the tree? It is for me. I feel deprived if I don't get at least one or two nice things. And I hate myself for feeling that way. At Christmas! When I'm supposed to be thinking about Jesus in the manger, and how I can help others! Still, there it is.

Money, child-rearing, tradition, religion, gift-giving: You will notice that these are not exactly small things. And on Christmas, you're expected to process them—as well as a buzzing swarm of other issues—*in one day*.

Remind me again why we're supposed to look forward to Christmas?

For someone who has always loved Christmas, I certainly spent a lot of years going insane over it. I baked double batches of seven kinds of cookies, oblivious to the fact that there are only four people in my immediate family. (I had vague notions of carrying beautifully decorated cookie platters to the neighbors, but never got around to it.) I made gingerbread houses, agonizing over the finer points of gumdrop window trimmings. I directed my church's Christmas pageant, roasted suckling pigs, and bought stocking stuffers for the dogs. I thought I was enjoying the whole thing. But come January, I was faced with the all-too-familiar feeling that I'd "flunked" Christmas yet again.

It's not supposed to be like this. It doesn't have to be like this. And I'm going to help you *stop* it from being like this.

If Only in My Dreams

A few years out of college, my boyfriend and I were setting up our new apartment with various hand-me-downs and flea market treasures. I was especially looking forward to Christmas this year, because we were so broke.

When my family gathered for Christmas, we opened our gifts in turn. I watched in envy as my sister-in-law opened exquisite and expensive gifts from my mother. My gifts from my mom were four cotton henleys from the Gap along with assorted Tupperware and a set of wooden spoons.

I asked my mother what the hell she had been thinking. Both my sister-in-law and her husband were successful lawyers. Here I was living like a pauper, and I had really wanted something nice. My mother explained that she had just trying to choose something appropriate for our individual "lifestyles." Great. She had decided to perpetuate my "lifestyle" of poverty and deprivation.—P. H. G.

Time and again, when I described this book to people, they would say, "I *hate* Christmas." One friend even suggested that that's what I should call the book. The people who were saying this were generally nice, kind, and happy. But Christmas does something to even the best of us. We *want* to love it unconditionally, but it keeps testing our love and patience every year.

*   *   *

I'll admit it. It was a quote in a Jane Brody column that first made me wonder why I was whizzing around so much. Her words were simple, but they really hit home: "Your children would rather have you spend time with them than bake them another batch of cookies."

I must have read things like that before. I had certainly heard them from my husband for the whole time we'd been married. (And just brushed them off as so many attempts to trip me up.) But for some reason, this time the quote hit me in the face like a wet washcloth. I actually remember flinching as I read it.

Because of course it was true. I was really baking the cookies for *myself*, not for the kids. A batch of hazelnut crescents meant another item to cross off the long, long list I had set up for myself—another way to prove that I really knew how to celebrate the holidays right. It had nothing to do with what was actually fun for me or the children. In fact, the kids often interrupted my work to ask when I'd be done with whatever Christmas chore I was laboring at so that I could play with them. I'd answer something like, "What are you talking about? It's *Christmas*! I have to put up this garland/mold this marzipan fruit/bake this saffron bread/polish this silver/crochet this hamster-stocking to make *you* happy!"

I'm not saying that Christmas is only for children—but the problem with the Christmas chores was that *no one* was benefitting from them except my To Do list. At least half of all my racing around was due entirely to compulsion.

All that has changed now. An outsider might not notice too many differences. I still bake cookies, trim the tree, get behind in my wrapping, try new crafts that don't work, and spend too much. But I *will* say I have fun doing it now, and I know my family has more fun. It took awhile for me to pare things down to where they were nutty without being insane (if I'm making myself clear). But I did it, and you can, too.

I promise I won't give you fuzzy suggestions about "feeling the spirit" and "taking time for joy" in this book. The advice I'll give you is more realistic and straightforward than that.

The fact is, over the past few years, I've gone from worrying about Christmas to loving it again. If that can happen for me, it can happen for you.

Maybe even with a little joy thrown in.

2

Sleep in Heavenly Peace

the absolute first most important christmas change you must make right away

O ye, beneath life's crushing load,
Whose forms are bending low,
Who toil upon the climbing way
With painful steps and slow,
Look now! for glad and golden hours
Come swiftly on the wing;
O rest beside the weary road
And hear the angels sing!

—EDWARD HAMILTON SEARS, "IT CAME UPON THE MIDNIGHT CLEAR"

Being unable to think incrementally is my worst affliction. It keeps me from ever doing *anything*. I call this trait the Mushroom Factor.

Pretend I want to clean my office (and that *would* be pretending, since I haven't touched it in six years). First, I suppose, I should get rid of the raggedy heaps of papers lying on the floor that I have to ski over even to get to my desk. But some of those papers are letters sent to me a few years back. Shouldn't I answer them first? Isn't it more important to keep up human connections than to priss around about cleanliness? I'd better find my stationery. But the stationery shelf is so dusty that I can't even think about writing any letters until I've dusted it. As if I even know where a dust cloth *is*; I'd better go buy one. On the other hand, why would I dust before I've tackled some of the bigger stuff? . . . Clearly, it's all impossible. Back to bed!

You get the idea. So when I tried to come up with the absolute first most-important change you need to make in your Christmas celebration this year, it took me a few days to work through the Mushroom Factor and winnow everything down. Tendrils of distraction kept creeping in. Say, for example, that I told you to stop wrapping your Christmas presents. Well, then, where would you store them? Under the bed? Wouldn't that mean you'd have to vacuum under there, and isn't extra vacuuming exactly what you *shouldn't* have to think about at Christmas?

That kind of thing.

And then I suddenly remembered a passage from Astrid Lindgren's wonderful book *Mischievous Meg*. This is a story— now out of print, alas—about a girl in Sweden and her family. One chapter is devoted to Christmas. On Christmas Eve, the family is sitting in front of the fire:

> Meg glanced anxiously at Mother to see if she was tired, but fortunately Mother was happy and not at all tired. Everyone had to be happy, and everyone had to feel that Christmas was wonderful, or something was spoiled for Meg. She had kept on saying to Mother, when she was working on the Christmas preparations, "You have to promise not to be tired on Christmas Eve."
>
> "Now, how *could* I be tired on Christmas Eve?" Mother had asked.

How indeed? we may sneer to ourselves. What with the shopping and the wrapping and the jillion other minutiae we're expected to orchestrate at Christmas, promising not to be tired seems like lunacy. But in fact, that's it. That's the number-one most important change you can make this year.

Make sure you're not tired at Christmastime

Okay, it's a nice theory—but easier said than done, you're now saying with a sob in your voice.

Very few of us are sitting around waiting for more to do. Rare is the person who thinks, "Excellent! Christmas is here! At last a way to fill those empty hours!" Usually Christmas adds many hours of work to a schedule that is already *plenty* jammed, thank you. We can't slice the other tasks out of our life, so we decide to sleep a little less, or race around a little more, or both.

This decision usually starts out being kind of fun, in a manic way. Why not wait until everyone else is asleep before you start baking? It will give you a clear two hours all to yourself, and the family will be greeted with beautiful cookies first thing in the morning—as if elves had visited your kitchen in the night. Just watching the smiles on their faces (the family's, not the elves') will make up for the lack of sleep, won't it?

Sure, for a while. But these things are cumulative. By the time Christmas Eve Day rolls around, you're barely on your feet, and you haven't even started thinking about Christmas dinner. There's an avalanche of wrapping left to do. And what if Santa is bringing your children toys that need to be assembled after the children are in bed?

For years I staggered home from the midnight Christmas Eve service to find my husband buried in Christmas assemblage—the final tipping point into helpless exhaustion. I know you've all gone through this. It's a Christmas cliché. You open a box to find twelve pounds of miscellaneous half-inch plastic segments that need to be clicked together to become a Playmobil dollhouse or Ninja Turtle Superdome; on completing the job at 2:15 A.M., you realize that you must now place seventy-five stickers with meticulous precision to make the toy look half recognizable.

Meanwhile, your spouse is hissing whispered curses as he tries to jam the rocking-horse handles through the horse's head or lurches across the living room with the new half-ton TV. (That was the year that Daddy hurt his back and had to spend all of Christmas Day in bed.) And then, suddenly, it's six in the morning—the hour at which your children are allowed to come flying into your bed screaming with excitement, which is not to say they haven't been thundering around for an hour and a half in their own rooms, waiting to be allowed to "wake up." By quarter after six you're sick with exhaustion, and there's still a whole churning, feverish day ahead of you.

How can I find the time to rest at Christmas?

I happen to be a master at sneaking any spare minute I can find to rest. Once, while singing in a Christmas concert, I managed to squeeze in a nap backstage during intermission, on the floor in my black dress and pearls, while the other chorale members milled around me. But some of the following ideas might work even better than falling asleep on the floor. What follow are some general concepts that, incorporated gradually, can change the way you celebrate Christmas as well as helping you to feel more like yourself and less like a sodden mattress. We'll get to more specifics in later chapters.

Don't carry out every tradition every year

Was there ever a real period in Christmas history when families accomplished as much as they do in Tasha Tudor stories? Trooping into the woods to find the perfect tree . . . stringing popcorn and cranberries to trim it . . . caroling at the houses of shut-ins . . . baking thirty kinds of cookies for the neighbors . . . making wreaths . . . making a gingerbread house . . . pulling taffy . . . cleaning the house from top to bottom . . . drinking eggnog in front of the fire . . . reading *A Christmas Carol* together . . . midnight Mass . . . that traditional Christmas Eve

Above Thy Deep and Dreamless Sleep...

Every Christmas Eve, our family all gets together and has a family Mass at 10:30 P.M. in the living room. (One of my uncles is a priest.) It's rather comfortable—more so than church. One year, during the Mass, we could see Mom's head drooping down and realized that she had fallen asleep sitting on the couch. When we all stood to exchange the Peace, my mother woke up. (For the uninitiated: During the exchange of the Peace, you're supposed to kiss or shake hands with the people around you and say "The Peace of the Lord be always with you;" the other person answers "And also with you.") Seeing people shaking hands and kissing, Mom jumped to her feet, took my aunt's hand, and said, "Hey, thanks for having us! Merry Christmas!"—D. G.

dinner . . . that traditional Christmas morning breakfast . . . that traditional Christmas dinner . . .

This on top of shopping, wrapping presents, and traveling—all in the two weeks that most schoolchildren get for Christmas vacation and the two or three *days* that are what most working adults take off for Christmas? If you add up the number of hours all this stuff will take and compare it with the number of hours you actually have, you will instantly notice a hemorrhaging time deficit that can't possibly be stitched shut.

And what about simply hanging out with the family? You can't be pushing yourself and the kids through holiday projects all day long; everyone will fray. A big part of any family holiday—perhaps the biggest part—should be devoted to enjoying unstructured time together.

Christmas traditions should not be a list that you go down, grimly checking off each item. Pick two or three essential traditions that seem to matter the most, depending on the size and age of your family, and save the rest for another year.

In my own family, for example, the kids are ancient adolescents who have recently developed a strong aversion to trimming the tree. For the past couple of years we've had an amazing amount of trouble even scheduling a time we'll all be in the house together. Two years ago, while we were hanging the ornaments, my then-eighteen-year-old daughter, Laura—home for the first tree-trimming since leaving for college—suddenly blurted out, "Isn't this *ever* going to be done?"

"People who don't have as many ornaments as we do would be finished by now," I answered.

"They are soooooooooooooooooooooooooo lucky," she moaned.

"The weird thing is that the tree would actually look better with just lights and no ornaments," said my son, John.

"I know." Laura sighed. "But what are you going to do?"

We've traveled a long way from the days when Laura wanted every single construction-paper cardinal and macaroni chain she'd ever made to be hung on the front of the tree where everyone could see them. But I can remember being the age she is now. I felt that the house should look Christmas-y enough that I'd have a nice backdrop as I was being picked up by friends to go somewhere more interesting. I certainly didn't want to be *in* the house savoring the beauty. Since John will be eighteen next Christmas, it's likely he'll be moving in the same direction. So next year either I'm trimming the tree by myself or we're just going to put up lights and leave the ornaments off. Even a "sacred" Christmas task as this may need to be skipped once in a while. If the kids discover that they miss doing it, fine! That will make the job more interesting the following year.

You *can* manage to skip a tradition or two this year without dropping dead. You want your children to think Christmas is something they carry inside them, not something that can only "arrive" when every last expected activity has been carried out. And you want them to realize that "But we always—" is not an automatic reason for doing something.

Resist the urge to augment—for this year, at least

Have you noticed that every year, the Christmas decorations in your neighborhood get more elaborate? Two years ago, the Mayhews only put lights on their apple tree. Last year, they added a lighted wreath to their front door. This year, they've also installed some of those weird grazing deer made out of baskets, or whatever that wicker-y stuff is. Next year, the deer will probably also be covered with lights. . . .

You're not imagining this. The national trend is toward more and more and more and more Christmas decorations. In her book *Why People Buy Things They Don't Need,* author Pam Danziger says that there are about 104 million American households—of which about a quarter add to their ornaments, lights, and decorations every year. Fifteen million of these households are "dedicated Christmas collectors" that add to their collections of "ornaments, villages, figurines, nutcrackers, nativities and dinnerware" every year. Christmas decorating is unique to the United States, says Danziger. "No other country, not even our closest neighbor to the north, Canada, goes in for the exuberant outdoor decorating and gift-giving that Americans do."

Great.

My friends Barry and Rux moved into an old Vermont farmhouse to discover that the previous owners had been fanatical Christmas decorators who had turned the house into a landmark every December. Unfortunately, these same previous owners were now building a house next door. "You'll still put up all the lights, right?" they asked hopefully. Rux explained that they would not, in fact she and Barry would be

Giddyap. Giddyap. Giddyap. Let's Go. Let's Look at the Show

The one-upping gets worse and worse. We went to a party where there was a fourteen-foot artificial tree. The hostess took me down the hall and showed me a fifteen-foot closet she'd had specially built so they could wheel the tree in on a trolley to store it during the year.—C. O.

fleeing Christmas by flying to Jamaica. The previous owner said, "Well, we still have all the lights. How 'bout if I come on over and set them up for you?"

Even though I scorn this trend, I can't help being nudged by it emotionally. In my town, all the Christmas stuff goes up on the Sunday after Thanksgiving—which means all the wreaths are up by Monday morning, sneering at me as I stumble bleary-eyed to the grocery store. I don't want to buy a wreath before Thanksgiving, so I never have mine ready—and I always feel guilty about it. What if people driving by my house think I'm not doing my bit? I keep track of their houses, so surely they're keeping track of mine! And look, the Havers have added lights to their wreath this year, and put candles in *all* their windows instead of just the first-floor ones! Oh, my God, I can't keep up!

If you find yourself becoming a prey to this hysteria, take a deep breath and remind yourself that although "more stuff" may appear to mean "more Christmas," it also means "more stuff to put away *after* Christmas."

Pay someone to help

One reason you're staying up too late may well be that you're looking for more time to *yourself*—not just more time in general. (Though of course a twenty-seven-hour-day would come in handy in December.) It's impossible to get certain Christmas chores done with children in the room. A good way to un-exhaust yourself is to get a baby-sitter to stay right in the house with you while you work your Christmas magic.

For several years, my husband and I used to hire a baby-sitter to play with the kids downstairs while we wrapped presents upstairs. This idea works for any Christmas chore, of course, not just wrapping packages. You can also hire a sitter to keep the kids out of the kitchen while you bake cookies—or to bake cookies with the kids while you put the lights on the tree. Or to watch a Christmas video with the kids while you address some Christmas cards.

Or to address the cards herself! Lots of middle-school and high-school kids would love to take baby-sitting wages for chores you may be sick of: wrapping presents, addressing envelopes in their little-circles-over-the-I's-handwriting, untangling the strings of lights, and replacing any missing bulbs. For the cost of having two presents wrapped by a mail-order company, you can buy an hour of a teenager's time. In December, that's better than finding a diamond in the snow.

But now you may be saying, "Yes, but Christmas is a time I should be *with* the kids, not hiring someone else to do it." Most children, though, don't mind having a baby-sitter watch them while their parents are in the house. As long as *you're* still home, having a sitter around is often like a playdate for kids. They may even decide that it's extra-Christmas-y to have you producing nice baking smells in the kitchen while they watch *How the Grinch Stole Christmas* with Leah in the living room.

What kids really don't like is to have their parents *leave* them with a sitter, which plays nicely into my next sleep-saver.

Don't go to any parties between December 10 and New Year's Eve
Unless you like parties, of course. But for many of us, they're the last straw at Christmas. You can see your friends anytime. Why do it during the busiest month of the year—which also

happens to be the family-est month of the year? Why eat even more than you're already going to be eating, and rack up even more social obligations, and force yourself to stay up even later wrapping presents?

Knowing that you won't have to go anywhere for the last two weeks before Christmas is wonderfully liberating. It frees up two or three evenings right away, giving you six or seven bonus hours (during which you can just stay in your pjs). It also sends an important message to your children: For them, knowing that they can count on having you home every evening of those last two weeks is a wonderful present.

You don't have to tell the people who've invited you why you're not coming. In fact, you probably shouldn't. There's something about the statement "I'm putting my family first" that suggests your host and hostess are not putting *their* family first. Saying "To save time, I'm not coming to your party" is obviously out of the question. But there's nothing wrong with *having* those reasons, as long as you don't share them.

You can tell your kids, though. Otherwise they might not even notice what they're supposed to be grateful for.

Also, never schedule routine appointments—teeth cleanings, checkups, and so on—for December. If

Up on the Housetop...

I remember being very small (about seven), trying to stay awake and see Santa despite all instructions and warnings. It was hard to sort out the various noises, none of which sounded like reindeer on the roof—but what did I know? Then, clear as a bell, a loud crash with assorted accompanying crashes, and my father's voice . . . downstairs, not asleep the way we were all supposed to be. And he said, "Dammit, Kitty, why did you put the roller skates there!?!" —Ah. The hoped-for roller skates.—J. V. M.

you've already done so (a lot of time these appointments are made months in advance), cancel them right away and reschedule them for January.

Want to give yourself the sensation of saving even more time? Make a few appointments for December, dread them for a little while, and then cancel them.

Keep in mind that Christmas does not begin and end on December 25

This one is too important not to have its own chapter. Turn a few pages and read Chapter Four: "Don't Open Presents on Christmas Day: And Other Radical Ideas for Spreading Christmas a Little Thinner." But not until you've taken everything in *this* chapter to heart.

Funnily enough, you may find you actually miss your traditional Christmas exhaustion at first. Many people get so used to this feeling that its absence makes them feel incomplete; it's akin to the phenomenon familiar to stress-relief consultants, who often find that what their clients actually want is to learn how to manage even *more* stress. But bear with your insecurity for a couple of Christmases, starting this year. Once you've realized how much healthier it feels to be well-rested—and how much more fun it makes your holidays—you'll never want to return to your old frantic ways.

And once you're not as tired, you'll have the energy to turn to the rest of this book and see how you can make Christmas even nicer for yourself.

3

Never Make Your Own Wrapping Paper

and the other christmas changes you must make right away (in order of importance)

A day or two ago,
the story I must tell,
I went out on the snow
and on my back I fell;
A gent was riding by
In a one-horse open sleigh,
He laughed as there I sprawling lie,
But quickly drove away.
—JAMES LORD PIERPONT, "JINGLE BELLS"

Let's assume you're just waking up from a nice nap on the sofa. You've already absorbed the lesson of the previous chapter: not letting yourself get too tired. Nice beginning, but you're not done yet. You're still carrying a big Santa sack weighted down with Christmas burdens—burdens you may have become so used to carrying that it's never occurred to you that you can put them down once in awhile. Maybe it's also never occurred to you to make your own wrapping paper (we'll get to that later), but I'm *certain* that there are other chores you can manage to shed, along with a lot of mental baggage. And it's the mental baggage we'll attack first: specifically, the idea that at Christmastime, you need to put everyone else's needs ahead of your own.

If the whole holiday comes down on your shoulders—or

you feel as if it does—then those shoulders had better be well taken care of.

If you are the main Christmas planner in your household, put yourself first

This may seem to run counter to all your best instincts. "Christmas is about caring for others more than ourselves," you're saying right now. Or, "Christmas is for children." Or, "If I really put myself first, we'd just sit on a beach some-where. No, *I'd* just sit on a beach somewhere, alone, wiggling my toes in the sand."

All right, then. Put yourself first *within reason*. Of course you're interested in making Christmas work, or you wouldn't be reading this book at all; you'd be out there on that beach while your family pitifully tried to struggle along without you. But here you are, still at home! That proves that you're already actually putting your family first, doesn't it?

Good. Now that we've established what a nice person you are, we can start establishing your Christmas Rights.

If you feel like changing a tradition, go ahead

If you're the one who maintains the traditions in your house—cooks specific foods, decorates the house, buys the presents—you have the ultimate say in whether they take place or not. And if your family is determined that certain traditions be carried out as usual, your family should be in charge of them, not you.

I have a friend—let's call her Pam—for whom the Mid-night Mass on Christmas Eve is the last straw. After a seven-course fish dinner with her extended family, they're all expected to pile into their coats and rush to church. When they get back home, her teenagers always disappear to wrap their presents for Christmas morning, leaving her to clean up the kitchen.

I suggested that either she skip the midnight service, or that the family go to the afternoon service instead. Pam looked at me as if I'd suggested she yank the cross off the altar and throw it out the window. "But we all love the Midnight Mass!" she wailed.

Well, then, skip the huge dinner beforehand.

"But that's when the whole family gets together!"

So cut back on some of the courses.

"But those are our family's traditional foods!"

Then the whole family should be helping clean up afterwards. Or you could switch to paper plates.

"But paper plates on Christmas Eve are tacky!"

Pammy, I'm losing patience here! Stop trying to find reasons to keep yourself miserable! *You have as much right to a happy Christmas Eve as your children do.* A tradition is not worth sustaining if it's meaningful to everyone in the family but you. What kind of message does it send to your kids—especially your daughters—if they see that Mom's main Christmas function is to be trampled by everyone else?

If you don't want to travel on Christmas, don't

Oh, boy, am I going to get into trouble with this one. But I think I'm right.

When Laura was six months old, we traveled to my parents' house for Christmas. (We live quite a distance from both sets of parents.) It was a nicely nutty visit in lots of ways. There were so many people staying in the house that all the stockings broke the cord they were hanging from and ended up in a heap on Christmas morning. Laura wasn't interested in any of her presents, preferring to fill an old tin measuring cup with drool. My brother-in-law washed his contact lens down the bathroom drain, so he, David (my husband), and my father got to take a sink apart. My parents' dog, Molly, got weird purplish splotches on her stomach. The vet thought they might

Rockin' Around the Christmas Tree

A Christmas that I still remember, and my mother probably does too, was when I was eight or nine. I enviously watched my older brother and sister unwrap very grown-up-looking stereos with separate turntables, tuners, speakers, and wood-grained sides. I then opened up a little red plastic record player that my parents had given me to be equitable. They were very pleased with themselves for having found something really cool for me, too, but it looked to me like a pre-school Kenner Close 'N Play. I was totally hurt and started to cry. The rest of my Christmas was ruined (at least for the next hour or two).
—J. E. O.

be caused by eating pistachios in the shell, and asked that we get pee and poop samples and check them for blood. I tried to catch some of Molly's pee in a coffee scoop fastened to an unbent clothes hanger, but the results were inconclusive.

Good times, good times. But on top of everything else, this was also when Laura was at the height of her "stranger anxiety." She did manage to develop a fervent crush on her uncle Mark; in all the pictures, you can see her making goo-goo eyes at him. But the sight of anyone outside the family made her burst into screams of fear and resentment. My parents' friends were naturally eager to lay eyes on the first grandchild in the family, so there were plenty of visitors, and Laura—who is the most stubborn person on earth—kept up her screams for pretty much the whole visit. At one point I had a little screaming fit myself.

"We're never coming here for Christmas again!" I blurted out after one particularly strident hour. And, so far, we never have. That's not because I still carry a grudge, but because David and I realized that when you have small children, Christmas is the *worst* time of year to travel. And no one has a chance for a nice relaxed visit anyway. The kids' routine gets all wrenched around, and no one is at her best. A visit at a less hectic time of year may be less "meaningful," but it will be more fun, and that makes more sense. (Which is, in turn, more meaningful.)

But what if your parents want to see their grandchildren at Christmas? This is often the case when the children are still young and adorable. So your parents should come to *your* house. They're not the ones who have to travel with kids!

David and I actually made a schedule. One set of parents would visit one year; the other set of parents the next year; the third year, the four of us would be on our own. This seemed the fairest: a set routine that never came to feel too hidebound.

I do realize that my own children will expect me to visit them on Christmas if I want to see them. That's fair. I've had plenty of Christmases in this house. When it's my turn to travel (if I want to), I'll be looking forward to it.

I also realize that some people will think I'm being selfish about all this. I can live with that. I'd much rather have people think I'm selfish than not have fun at Christmas. I realize, too, that many extended families live closer to one another than mine does, and many people like big gatherings more than I do. (I'd rather concentrate on just a few people at a time.) So feel free to dash this book to the ground in disgust if what I'm saying makes no sense to you. But then think about how comfy you'd feel waking up in your own bed this Christmas. . . .

Question all your Christmas assumptions to be sure they make sense

The main thing people wrongly assume about Christmas is that it should be fun all the time. Why? Just because you want it to be? You've surely learned by now that you can't compel fun.

You can never rely on your kids (or yourself) to have a good time on important occasions. You might have spent weeks planning a wonderful Christmas for them only to hear that one miniscule glitch has destroyed the day. When I was growing up, a constant holiday refrain was that my brother, Ned, the only boy after three girls, had once again "wrecked everything." He opened his presents too fast, or too slowly, or he didn't string the popcorn daintily enough, or he got mad because someone else had finished off the ribbon candy instead of letting him do it. Poor Ned had only to sit down on the wrong chair to have my sisters and I tell him he'd wrecked Christmas again. Obviously this wasn't true except from our point of view, and even then the wreckage was only temporary. I hope my parents just ignored it.

The Christmas Spirit doesn't hover around sprinkling you with a continuous shower of Christmas Dust. It comes and goes—for kids as well as adults. When it shows up, you welcome it. When it calls in sick, you just keep plugging along and reminding yourself that an event like Christmas is *worthwhile* even when it's not always fun.

Rethink the presents

For example: Despite the way you may feel, not everything about Christmas has to be "even." Are you giving someone a present simply because she gave you a present last year? If so, why? Will her feelings be hurt if she doesn't get a present from you? Would it hurt to ask her? Maybe she'd like to give fewer presents and is only giving you one because you gave her one.

Similarly, there's no reason to give a present to someone just because *you* gave *him* a present last year. Who says you have to keep it up forever? Maybe you'll give him one next year, maybe not. For years, several friends and I exchanged little Christmas presents—cookies or ornaments, that kind of thing. Then, as our kids got older and we didn't see each other as often, the custom began to sputter. You'd get a tin of candy

And Mamma in Her Kerchief

In the Wall Street boom years, we were invited to a Christmas pajama party for which guests were told that they were "required" to come in their nightwear. (The invitation, of course, was a reworking of "The Night Before Christmas.") We had a few other parties that night, so we didn't come in pajamas. The hostess met us at the door and said we had to go home and come back in our jammies. A crowd of people, all holding shot glasses, gathered behind her to holler that we were party poopers and that they would "strip us naked" if we didn't dress appropriately. We went on to the other parties instead.—S. H.

from someone and feel you had to "retaliate" before the week was out. Or you'd have a spurt of energy, drop off batches of cookies everywhere, and come home feeling you'd actually imposed on some of your friends because they felt bad about not having something ready for you.

Which was silly. You didn't care, right? You just felt like giving away some cookies. And if your friends had been the ones giving you the cookies, they wouldn't have minded if you hadn't had a little present ready to whisk into their hands. If they *had* minded—well, I don't want to sound like a mom, but then they wouldn't really have been your friends. But if they thought about it at all, the most they probably felt was a comfortable sense of superiority over you. And that, my friends, IS the spirit of Christmas.

Well, no, it's not, but it won't kill you. Let them have their little glow of satisfaction. That can be your present to them this year.

Sometimes it works to formalize a non-present-giving agreement. My siblings and I, and David and his siblings, decided long ago to stop giving one other Christmas presents. We were all stretched to the limit in terms of both time and money. None of us needed more objects, more clothes, more Christmas decorations, more anything; none of us needed more thank-you notes to (not) write. The people who cared were our kids, so why not give presents only to the nephews and nieces? Then David and his sister and brother decided to stop doing even that. This shocked me a little, but it wasn't up to me, was it? And all the cousins on that side of the family still seem to be alive.

My sister and her family, and her husband's parents and siblings and *their* families, all live in Los Angeles. Every year they put all the adults' names, and each adult picks another adult to "gift." I think this would be a lot of fun, though it's not as easy to organize if you all live in different cities. But a friend of mine with six brothers and sisters, all widely scattered across the country, has somehow managed to figure that part of it out. They all pick one sibling or spouse and give that person a filled stocking. I like that idea as well.

Like a Bowlful of Jelly

Rich was very pleased with himself this year. He had done all the shopping for his petite girlfriend without any help. He was beaming when she unwrapped the boxes of clothing in front of her family. She opened the first of the several boxes and saw that it was labeled "Lane Bryant." Inside was a huge gray wool V-neck sweater. After she had opened box after box filled with size 46–48 clothing, it became clear that this was not a mistake. Rich, still not recognizing any error, said, "Well, I know you like your clothes big."
—K. R.

And stop buying presents for your children's teachers, for heaven's sake! My mother was a teacher for many years. When

I asked her how she'd felt about Christmas presents from her students, she wrote back:

> I had mixed feelings. I think parents felt obligated to buy or make things, and that wasn't a good thing for many of them, I imagine, at a busy and costly time of year. Sometimes, however, older students—eleventh or twelfth grade—made or bought very thoughtful presents: something from the kiln, something they'd baked, some book that they thought I would enjoy. It's the competitiveness that's bad, and that probably happens mostly in the lower school and among the parents.

Agreed. Ideally, you'd write each teacher a lovely note saying how much his or her time with your child meant to you. In practice, you're unlikely to have the time, and besides it's hard to write that kind of letter without feeling self-conscious. (I always worry that I'll sound as though I'm begging for good grades for my children.)

At the school my kids went to, there's a good holiday custom. Parents—I mean, parents who want to do this; no one has to—are asked to buy as many identical small presents as there are teachers and staff in their child's grade. And I mean really small presents—stocking-stuffer level. Tangerines, candy, packets of cocoa, cute seasonal packs of Kleenex, and so on. Then the items are divided up and each staff member is given a Christmas bag with all the items in it. Although this custom does require a few sturdy P. T. O.–type parents to organize the whole thing and prepare the bags, it has many advantages:

- ✩ Everything's anonymous, so there's no vying to see which parent can give the teacher the best present.

- ✩ The whole school staff can be included, not just the teachers.

- ✩ No one has to write thank-you notes.

Anyway, I think you get the idea: Presents are not an automatic requirement every year; they're not an automatic quid pro quo; and most adults probably don't care about getting them as much as you might think.

But wait, that doesn't include you! *You* have to make sure you get a few things you really like! Which leads to something you absolutely must do.

Get some Christmas presents for yourself

And wrap them, and put them under the tree with a note, just as you do with everyone else's presents.

I realize this sounds pathetic. And—well—okay, it is. *But it works.*

It's perfectly appropriate to give yourself a little reward while you're giving so much to so many other people. How else are you going to be sure you have the new mystery novel you've been wanting, or a nice pair of earrings? You don't have to go nuts, but as long as you're buying stuff for everyone else, go ahead and include yourself; it will make a surprising difference, and you'll feel much better taken care of at this demanding time of year.

You can't just buy your presents and start using them right away, of course. You must wait until Christmas, like everyone else. That's what makes this a selfless act instead of a selfish one.

I always write "To a GREAT MOM, with love from Mom" on the tags for my own presents. Now, *that's* pathetic. But somehow when I read the tags on Christmas morning, I feel as patted on the back as if someone else had written the tags, not me. I'll take it, pathetic or not.

Keep a Christmas notebook

This isn't adding something to your list of chores; it's helping to take a lot of them away. I promise.

Get a nice red or green spiral notebook. Have your children decorate it with stickers if they want. Keep it in the kitchen during December, and somewhere you can get at it easily the rest of the year if you have sudden Christmas inspirations (for good presents, especially). And use it to jot down every Christmas detail you think might be helpful for this year and future years.

Here are some of the things you should keep track of:

☆ The dates you order presents online or from catalogs. (Don't list the kids' presents here unless they're in code. Hiding your Christmas notebook would defeat its purpose.)

☆ The dates you mail out packages.

☆ Recipe ideas that do or don't work. If you try a new recipe and love it, write down which book or section of your recipe file it's in. If you try a new recipe and hate it, make sure to note that as well, so you won't waste time on it again.

I almost always make almond buttercrunch to give away as Christmas presents. I've memorized the recipe, so I never go to my cookbook for it. That's why, one year, it finally occurred to me to make a note of the fact that if you try to make five times the recipe for buttercrunch and the candy crystallizes, you're going to have a lot of wrecked candy sitting around that only your children, because they are wrong, will like better than regular buttercrunch. "Make only 2X," I wrote. Then, because I was certain that the following year I would think, "Yeah, but if I quintuple the recipe it will be faster," I added, "*2X truly actually faster.*"

And finally, last *and* least:

Never make your own wrapping paper

Although handmade wrapping paper does make a good present in itself—especially one your children can give to, say, their grandparents—it's a crime to work on a beautiful, time-consuming project that will just be thrown away. From an ecological point of view, wrapping paper's a waste anyway; we should all be using old newspapers to wrap our presents (except that no one will). Purposely creating something that's meant to be discarded is insane.

No, wait! The *real* last and least suggestion for having a smoother, more enjoyable Christmas is not to lose a crown on Christmas Eve by biting into some raspberry candy. I'm sure my husband would agree.

4

Don't Open Presents on Christmas Day

and other radical ideas for spreading
christmas a little thinner

She had a splendid Christmas all day. She ate so much candy that she did not want any breakfast; and the whole forenoon the presents kept pouring in that the expressman had not had time to deliver the night before; and she went 'round giving the presents she had got for other people, and came home and ate turkey and cranberry for dinner, and plum-pudding and nuts and raisins and oranges and more candy, and then went out and coasted and came back with a stomach-ache, crying; and her papa said he would see if his house was turned into that sort of fool's paradise another year; and they had a light supper, and pretty early everybody went to bed cross.

—WILLIAM DEAN HOWELLS, *CHRISTMAS EVERY DAY*

Have you ever noticed how many children put off getting sick until Christmas Eve or Christmas Day? I'm sure it's not a coincidence. Christmas is just as stressful for kids as it is for us. But in my family, Christmas improved 30 percent the year my daughter, Laura, then nine years old, got the flu on Christmas Eve. Laura was still so sick the next morning that, although she could languidly open presents, she didn't even want to think about eating. Since we had no company that year, I decided we would just postpone Christmas dinner until Laura was better.

It made a *huge* difference. For the first time since the kids had been born, I could just sit there and watch them open their presents—and then, when they were done unwrapping and ready to start playing, I was available. I didn't have to leap off the sofa and rush into the kitchen to start cooking. I didn't have to spend the afternoon washing load after load of dishes and peeling potato after potato while the kids kept coming in to say, "*Now* can you play with me?"

This was when the children were still young enough that some of their toys needed to be set up before they could even start playing—back in John's Lego-playing days, for instance. A six-year-old can't really get started on a huge Lego structure if there isn't a place cleared for him to do it, and our dining-room table was John's traditional Lego-playing spot. Until the year we put off Christmas dinner, he had always been out of luck on Christmas afternoons—just when he wanted to start building whatever big-ticket Lego set he'd gotten that morning, and just when *I* wanted the table to look ready for a photo shoot should any photographers happen to be spying on us.

Now, suddenly, the dining-room table was still bare—all ready for John to spread out all those millions of tiny plastic pieces. And now, suddenly, I didn't need David to help me in the kitchen while I raced around getting crankier by the second. David, who loves Legos himself, could just spend the afternoon puttering with John and convincing him that yes, alllllllll the pieces had been included, it was just a question of finding them. ("The Lego people didn't put that piece in the box!" was a constant refrain around our house when John was little.) Meanwhile, I could hang out with Laura. She was still feeling droopy, and if I'd been cooking Christmas dinner she would have had to spend a lot of time feeling droopy alone while poor David divided the hours between her, John, and an increasingly weepy wife.

Since I was able to put in both quantity and quality time with the children, I was also able to take a nap without feeling guilty. This meant that I didn't spend the rest of the day longing for Christmas to be *over* so I could drag myself to bed.

It's not as if we would have been hungry for Christmas dinner anyway. We always have a big Christmas Eve dinner, to start with. We always have a big protein-y breakfast on Christmas morning, much more than we normally eat, and then on top of that there's all the candy in the stockings. (I make sure to put the same amount in my own stocking as in the kids', naturally.) I had become used to waddling around the kitchen making Christmas dinner while I was already stuffed—one of the worst feelings to have when you cook—and then serving it to a family that wasn't even particularly eager to eat it.

Well, no more! It's been ten years since that Christmas, and we've never gone back to having Christmas dinner on the 25th. We always wait at least two or three days for it, and this past year we waited until January 2, when Laura had come back from a trip with her boyfriend's family.

Think about the advantages, besides not cramming the 25th with more activities than any family should have to handle:

☆ *You have one less thing to think about before Christmas Day.* You won't have to do dinner shopping on top of finding the stockings; wrapping the last-minute presents; racing to the mall to make up the deficit when you realize that one of your children has only half as many presents as the others; and taking the rabbits to the emergency rabbit vet forty-five minutes away on December 23. (In my house, we can count on one of the animals getting sick at every major holiday, as well as any morning we're leaving for a long vacation. Most recently, one of the rabbits developed something called, I swear, Floppy Rabbit Syndrome.)

☆ *You'll actually be hungry.* You can shop for your dinner ingredients, and cook the dinner, when you're more ready to face food again. You'll have gotten a second wind, and making the dinner will be more interesting.

☆ *You'll have more people available to help in the kitchen.* When your children are small, this can be a disadvantage, but you can always ask them to make a center-piece or draw place cards or something.

☆ *You can share the celebration.* Since everyone else you know will already be done with Christmas dinner (until everyone on earth owns a copy of this book and begins obeying my commands), you can invite friends or family members you might not normally be able to see at this time of year.

☆ *You have a major tradition to look forward to after the 25th.* This prevents Christmas from crashing to the ground with that sickening thud on the morning of the 26th.

Because—and this is very, very important—one of the best ways to improve Christmas is to *spread it thinner*.

Christmas should last more than one day

Why else have you been singing "The *Twelve* Days of Christmas" all these years? Just for fun? And how could that be fun anyway, since it's one of the most boring Christmas songs going—almost as boring as "The First Noel"? (Don't get me started on "The First Noel," except to beg that if you're going to make us sing it in church, please only make us sing three verses. It's the longest, most tedious song, and that melody! *Up* and back and *up* and back it crawls, like a windshield wiper.) Christmas is traditionally a twelve-day holiday, and it's lasted twelve days since well before Christ was born.

What I mean by that is that the early Mesopotamians celebrated a New Year's festival called Zagmuk, which lasted twelve days. So did a similar Persian and Babylonian festival called Sacaea. Thus, through various historical methods, a twelve-day celebration became associated with Christmas as well.

As you probably know already, there's no evidence that Jesus was born anywhere near December. And the stuff about

Tall in the Saddle We Spend Christmas Day...

Every New Year's Day, my former mother-in-law made a big deal of announcing the theme for next year's Christmas. She spelled it out in children's blocks on the mantel so that when we came down on New Year's morning, there it was. Themes included "Christmas in Cowtown" (Western, cowboys, cactuses), "Peace on Earth" (terra-cotta "pieces of earth," get it?), and "Winter Wonderland" (Vermont-ish). Then she'd spend all year looking for appropriate bric-a-brac and expecting her friends and family to do the same.

By Christmas, the work was done. Every ornament on the tree would reflect that year's theme. Who knew you could find so many terra-cotta ornaments? Every flat surface would have little displays—Mary and Joseph in Western garb, for example. The wrapping paper and porch decorations would have the same theme; even the drawers in the guest room would have sachets with cowboys lassoing a Christmas tree or whatever. When we arrived from out of town for Christmas, my mother-in-law, who always wore a super-large bow on the back of her hair, would be beside herself with excitement. She would jump up and down clapping her hands and screeching, "Come see my play pretties, come see my play pretties!"

She was a smart, energetic woman who unfortunately never found much useful to do with her talents.—A. S. M.

the manger was made up to make Jesus' birth echo the proph-
esies about the Messiah in the Old Testament. So there's
nothing particularly "real" about the choice of December 25
in the first place. Moreover, according to the Christian liturgical calendar, Christmas is supposed to start on December
25 and end on January 5. This means it's practically your *duty*
to spread it out.

In the olden days, when no one had any fun because they
were working all the time, a twelve-day festival meant you
spent most of the day cobbling or milling or whatever, and just
a part of the day frolicking. Now that we don't all live with
our extended families in tiny villages, most of us can't get together for measured amounts of festivities twelve days in a
row. But that doesn't mean we can't keep Christmas simmer-
ing for twelve days.

Open the presents before or after December 25—preferably after

I realize this is sacrilege. Not opening *presents* on *Christmas Day*?
I wouldn't dare to suggest it if it hadn't worked so well for my
own family.

On two separate occasions, we've taken ski trips with
other families that required our leaving on Christmas morning
itself. Rather than treat December 24 as "Present Day" when
we knew we'd have so much packing and running around to
do, we decided not to open anything until we'd come back
home.

Leaving our house without opening the presents was one of
the most liberating feelings in the world—for the children as
well as the adults. We had detached ourselves from what I suspect we all secretly considered the most important, most iron-
clad ritual of Christmas, and look! It hadn't turned out to be
nearly as important as we'd feared! We didn't miss it! We
were free! What's more, we still had the presents to look forward to when we came back.

No matter when you open the presents, open them *one at a time*, with everyone in the family taking turns as much as possible. (Of course adults usually have fewer presents under the tree than children do, so you probably won't be able to be completely strict about the turn-taking.) My husband knew a family where all the kids got up whenever they felt like it, opened their presents on their own, and then went on with their day. That seems horrible and alien to me. Almost as bad as a general free-for-all where the kids blitzkrieg the tree and rip their presents open while trampling to bits everything that isn't theirs. Taking turns not only makes the process more civilized but also stretches it out so that there seem to be more presents for everyone.

And that's all to the good, since even those among us who would like to de-emphasize the "present" aspect of Christmas can't honestly say they want fewer presents.

Here are a few suggestions for other things to reserve until the 26th or thereafter:

Holiday movies

They're generally more crowded before the 25th. Besides, come the 27th or 28th, you'll all be feeling claustrophobic and ready to leave the house. You can also save any Christmas videos or DVDs until after the big day. (For when you're ready to start feeling claustrophobic again, I guess.)

Christmas cards

Christmas cards are sort of a problem. Originally I was going to say you shouldn't send them at all.

But the truth is, I *love* getting holiday cards, especially the ones with pictures of people's children. Also, of course, newsletters. I wish someone would collect all the Christmas newsletters and publish a book of them. They would have to include the following, which we got from some acquaintances and which described (in poetry) the newest member of their family:

We used much of our savings by splurging on a car.
A Camry from Toyota seemed the wisest choice by far.
We rationalized our purchase by many devious means;
To enjoy the car is really all that matters in our schemes.

Anyway, I gluttonously collected other people's cards for many years, without getting around to sending any of my own. It's always something you're compelled to do when your kids are little and you can send their photos to deprived, deprived people who *must* be shown how cute they are. But then the kids

I Don't Know If There'll Be Snow, But Have A Cup of Cheer...

I was invited to a cookie swap by a dear friend several years ago. I was told to make fourteen dozen cookies. I was also urged to "make them look pretty and yummy." So I did. I made nine dozen meringue meltaway cookies and then got bored with that recipe and made another five dozen scrumptious raspberry thumbprint shortbread cookies. I packed each dozen in beautiful holiday cellophane and adorned each with red and green satin ribbons. In my opinion, I kicked ass in the baking department. I arrived feeling confident and even a little smug. I proudly laid my creations out on the table and stepped back. Then a woman approached me and yelped, "What did you do? You were supposed to make all of the same cookies! You didn't do it right!" All eyes turned toward this fiasco. These chicks were actually glaring at me! All because I had wanted to add a little variety to life.

I left, but not without taking my share of their cookies.—L. L.

grow up and become more resistant to the idea of posing, no matter how much Mom is capering around in the background trying to make them laugh. One year, I was able to make them pose because I had just sprained my ankle three minutes before that—while getting the camera—and was in obvious pain. But you can't count on hurting yourself every year.

And *then* there comes a time when the kids aren't even around that much, and you think, "But I can't send a card without a picture in it—what's the point?" The whole thing dwindles away, and so does the pile of cards you get each year as your friends either reach the same conclusion or delete you from their list.

My husband, who actually wrote a *New Yorker* article about greeting cards, says I'm wrong, and that more people than ever are sending Christmas cards. To which I can only answer, "Maybe so, but not people like us."

For several years in a row, I bought a few dozen cards and then sheepishly put them away in February when it became clear that they weren't going to be sent. (Observe the passive voice there. "They weren't going to be sent." Maybe I should just say, ". . . when it became clear that elves weren't going to help me send them.") One year, I sent out a mass mailing in March—just a single typed sheet with the following message. "Don't take us off your Christmas-card list! We're *trying* to get our cards under control." This bought me a few more years of inaction and useless card-buying. Finally, David said he wouldn't make the kids pose for any more Christmas card photos until I had written and addressed each card. Since I had always hoped, wrongly, that a stack of photos would guilt me into doing the cards, I gave up. (My sister Cathy also took photos of her daughters for several Christmases and then didn't get around to sending them. Last year, she finally sent out cards with dozens of old photos in each. She had to put a million stamps on the envelopes.)

But then a year ago we actually had both children in the same place at the same time, and we took a picture of them that came out so well that I couldn't resist sending out cards. (Laura thought her hair wasn't straight enough, but it was.) I had forgotten that writing cards and addressing envelopes could actually be a fun, soothing kind of busywork. An hour a day working away at it while watching old "West Wing" and "CSI" episodes, and the job was done in a week. Okay, two weeks, because some of those old episodes are really great. And the response we got was genuinely heartwarming. The majority of the recipients either e-mailed or wrote us to thank us. Writing a *letter* to thank someone for a *card*? I was amazed.

I saw that I had underestimated how much Christmas cards mean to your friends and family. Taking that into account, I don't have the heart to say this is a ritual worth getting rid of. Sending Christmas cards strengthens the bonds between people. I hate to sound mushy, but that's what Christmas is supposed to be about. Trimming less meaningful Christmas chores from your routine makes more sense.

But there's no reason at all that the cards need to go out before December 25. I notice that more and more friends are sending New Year's cards, which I hope takes hold as a custom. It's more secular; it prolongs the holiday feeling; and, not least, it will make your life in December a lot easier.

I would suggest that you send out cards at a totally different time of year—*Happy Arbor Day! Happy Summer Solstice!*—but I doubt anyone will start doing that, so forget it. But there's no reason not to make Valentine's Day your annual card-sending ceremony if January still seems too hectic. *No one* has any fun in February, so an annual Valentine would mean a lot—even more than a Christmas card, maybe.

New Year's Eve Activities

New Year's Eve—ugh, ugh, ugh. Worst holiday of the year by far. We never, ever go out for it; we always stay home with the kids. Actually, now that our kids are whirling in their own social universes, we always stay home with ourselves. And this past year, when both kids were out at parties, we celebrated by cleaning their bathroom together. (It really needed it.) But I would still rather have done that than gone to a New Year's Eve party.

There are two traditional New Year's Eve activities that kids love. The first is taking a bowl of ice water and dripping candle wax into it to predict what will happen to each person in the coming year. The shape your wax clumps in will give you "clues" about your fortune. You must be a little creative with your interpretation here; you must also be rather proactive with the way you drip the wax, making sure it falls in a definite clump. Otherwise you'd only be able to say "I predict that you will have . . . many small white dots floating around." But with some imagination, a clump of wax can be anything— a guinea pig, a new computer, Australia. ("Maybe you'll be going around the world!")

The second activity is actually writing out predictions for the year to come, and reading everyone's predictions from last year. Of course this depends on your being able to *find* everyone's predictions from last year. Keep them somewhere obvious, like on a string around your neck.

I always predict that one of the pets will have babies—and my prediction always comes true! It's a Christmas miracle!

Three Kings' Day, or The Feast of Epiphany

Although most Christmas pageants and nativity scenes put the Three Kings alongside the manger with everyone else, their arrival in Bethlehem is traditionally celebrated on January 6. The legend has it that the Three Kings—Caspar, Melchior, and Balthazar, also known as the Magi and the Wise Men—saw a bright star in the sky on the night of Christ's birth and followed it to Bethlehem.

When I was a child I thought a lot about this story. It seemed to me that following a star was no more reliable than following the moon, and I couldn't figure out how the Kings had managed it. I suppose it had something to do with celestial navigation, which seems just as impossible to me now as it did then. Anyway, they finally got there and presented their gold, frankincense, and myrrh to Jesus. Mary thanked them politely and said she would put the nice presents away until Jesus was old enough to appreciate them. Joseph rolled his eyes and thought, "Great. Another thing to pack."

When I was growing up, Epiphany was always the day my family took down the Christmas tree. As I've said elsewhere in this book, I like to leave the tree up for longer than that—and getting rid of the tree isn't very celebratory, in any case. In Mexico, January 6 was traditionally the day kids got their presents. They would leave their shoes out on the night of January 5, stuffing them with hay or grass for the Kings' camels, and in the morning the shoes would be filled with presents. (Another thing that bothered me as a child: in countries where the children left out their shoes, wouldn't the presents have to be shoe-sized or smaller? Maybe that was the point.)

You may feel there's been enough present-giving in the house by the time January 6 arrives, but it would still be a nice minor custom to have your children put their shoes out for a token present.

A Three Kings' Day cake is another fun tradition, one we always carried out when my children were small. You

I'm Getting Nuttin' for Christmas

When I was six, our big, shaggy French briard, Napoleon, realized that there was a wrapped bone under the tree for him and began wildly ripping apart a pile of presents to my parents from their friends. He shredded all the cards and wrapping to such an extent that Mom and Dad didn't have a clue as to which of their friends had given them what— a situation that caused Mom and Dad great distress, but created nothing but laughter for me. Of course it was all the funnier because Napoleon hadn't touched any of *my* presents.—D. L.

take a cake or a coffee cake and in it hide several small charms. (It's easiest to do this by inserting the charms in the bottom of the cake.) Traditionally, only a dried bean was hidden in the cake, and whoever found it was king for the day: A bad idea, in my opinion. First, it means that only one person gets to find the bean, and second, I once made a Three Kings' Day cake with a dried bean for my Sunday School, and one of the kids ate the dried bean. "I *thought* there was something kind of crunchy," he said.

What I do is take is some tiny silver charms that are supposed to be hidden in a plum pudding and put them in my cake instead. These are things like a tiny horseshoe (good luck!), a four-leaf clover (also good luck!), a wedding bell (a wedding!), and a thimble (lots of sewing in the New Year!). Wait, the thimble one can't be right. Let me check. . . . Oops, it doesn't mean lots of sewing; it means you won't get married in the coming year. You figure that one out. Some people suggest putting in a tiny plastic baby. Maybe it's just me, but I don't like the idea of biting down on a baby. But I can see where kids of a certain age would find it hilarious.

Anyway, put in whatever you want. Just make sure to warn people not to bite down too hard when you serve the cake. Make sure, too, that any small children in the house definitely get a charm in their piece of cake. It's demoralizing for little kids not to find anything at all. You can teach them about being good losers at a less important time of year.

5

The Santa Question

to believe or not to believe
(and what to tell the kids)

Here comes Santa Claus, here comes Santa Claus,
Right down Santa Claus Lane,
He doesn't care if you're rich or poor,
For he loves you just the same.
—GENE AUTRY, OAKLEY HALDEMAN

When I was three, my mother told me about Santa Claus. Who, by the way, does not live on a "lane," no matter what the song says.

"How can he come down the chimney when we don't have a chimney?" I asked. We lived in an apartment at the time.

"For people without chimneys, he comes through the door."

"How can he get through all those doors in one night?" I asked.

"You're right," said my mother. "There is no Santa Claus."

And that was the end of that.

There was never a time when Santa was part of my Christmas—or that of my next-in-line sister, Cathy. The two of us worked hard to disillusion our younger cousin Sarah when her family came to visit one Thanksgiving. I still remem-

Away in a Manger

My niece Emily was much put out at age four when her baby brother was getting too much attention as the official Baby Jesus in the living Nativity scene at church. (Emily had been assigned the part of an ox.) She managed to survive the Christmas Eve service, walked out to the car, closed the door, and announced, "Oh well, soon it will be Easter and they'll nail him to the cross."

—J. S.

ber how proud I was of the clever, subtle way I would casually bring up the topic. "Isn't it funny how some *little, little babies* believe in Santa?" I would remark. My aunt had to keep leaping into the conversation to drown me out.

Cathy and I were kind enough to let our youngest sister, Cornelia, and our brother, Ned, cling to their (as I saw it) pathetic fantasies for a few years. Older siblings are usually pretty nice about this. Even so, our parents must still have been uneasy about Santa, because Cornelia was terrified of him. Once she woke up crying that she'd heard the reindeer on the roof; another time, she woke up screaming that Santa was trying to come through the mirror.

Of course lots of children like the idea of Santa without actually wanting him to get near them. For one thing, he wears a costume, and many kids feel oogly about costumes. For another, they worry that he might be able to see into their heads. When my kids were little, my husband noticed that Mr. Rogers spent a lot of time on his show explaining that although Santa knows what you want for Christmas, "He doesn't know what you're thinking."

Then there's the way he just shows up without being invited. At my friend Jack's house, Santa actually walks right inside during waking hours and talks to the children. "Both of them are scared of him, and have repeatedly said that they don't want him to come to the house," Jack told me. After some negotiation—Jack's wife, Theresa, really likes wearing that Santa suit!—four-year-old Charlie said, "How about this, Dad. How about *you* talk to Santa, and I'll go upstairs. Or I'll just talk to him on the phone."

Two-year-old Max, the son of friends, caught a cold the day after Christmas and successfully worked out the difference between it and his Christmas presents: "Santa not give me a cold."

Having grown up without any Santa connection at all—positive or negative—I decided that our household should continue the Santa-free tradition. *My* children would never be tainted by false idolatry. They would know whom to thank for their presents. They would never wonder why Santa actually *does* seem to "care if you're rich or poor." (This is, indeed, Santa's most heartbreaking problem, and I wish I knew how to solve it. A friend of mine told her daughter that parents have to buy all the presents from Santa. That's not the solution, I'm pretty sure.) Ours would be a rational home.

But it turned out that my husband, David, had come from a family where St. Nick was a welcome guest. (Don't you hate it when writers try to work in synonyms for Santa? "Kris Kringle" is the worst one.) He left "Santa presents"—all the big-ticket items—prominently displayed in the living room. They were unwrapped and assembled, so you could tell right away what Santa had brought you; the more modest stuff from your parents was wrapped and waiting under the tree.

My friend Sarah raised her family on a similar principle. One year Sarah stayed up all night putting together a dollhouse from Santa. The next morning, her daughter Emily eyed the dollhouse and said, "Mom, no offense, but what did you and Dad give me?" In my husband's house, Santa's heavy responsibilities meant that sometimes he got behind and had to call in a neighbor to help him assemble the children's toys, and the two of them would get hammered while they tried to put the G.I. Joe fort together. Anyway, David was horrified when he heard that Santa might not exist for his own children.

"If you tell them there's no Santa," he said, "I'll tell them there's no God."

I caved immediately. But the "discussion" proved that even the most rational secular humanists have an irrational god-worshipping side. Because what was my husband doing in this case but trying to keep his own gods alive?

Santa Claus vs. God

There are surprisingly many similarities between Santa Claus and God. I'm not criticizing God here, by the way, so if you're planning to send me hate mail you should save a stamp. (God can take a joke.) And I'm not criticizing Santa either. I love Santa now that my husband's converted me. You should see my Santa Claus collection! I have over two hundred Santas! I even have a Santa who's in his workshop painting a lot of little tiny Santas!

But I do have to point out that many people treat God and Santa as if they're basically the same. Both God and Santa live somewhere "up there." Both of them reward you for good behavior and punish you for bad; you'll notice that hell is traditionally believed to be a lake of fire and Santa is traditionally believed to bring lumps of coal to those who have been bad. Both of them know when you are sleeping and know when you're awake. Both of them have loud, booming voices. Both of them receive prayers—what is a letter mailed to the North Pole but a prayer?—and both are medium-tall, with brown hair and glasses. Oh, no, wait, that's just God, or what I believed God looked like when I was little.

And if you don't want your kids to believe in one or the other—especially Santa—people are just appalled. Many of my friends were genuinely shocked and angry when I hinted that we might not make Santa part of our Christmas traditions. If I had told the same friends I wasn't planning to bring the kids up as Christians, they would have been *way* more tolerant.

"That's everyone's personal choice," they would have said, whether they approved or not. "I would never impose my own beliefs on another." But whisper that your kids might not believe in Santa and watch your friends drag out the belief-imposin' guns!

"You're taking away your child's innocence," they say—as if there's something particularly innocent about believing that a sack-carrying man in a red suit comes down the chimney in the middle of the night. "Every child needs something to believe in at Christmas." As if the whole Jesus-in-the-manger thing—more about this later—doesn't offer a big enough story. And as if something about getting presents, which is already pretty good, requires extra padding to make it even better.

The real problem

Then your friends will get to the part that really bothers them. "But if *your* kids don't believe in Santa, they'll tell *my* kids there's no Santa!"

Why should this present such a problem? Let's look at the God analogy again. Say you raise your child in one religion: Do you feel threatened when your child makes friends with a child of another religion? Of course not. (If you do, please close this book and go away.) You tell the child, "There are many different ideas about religion, and this is what *we* happen to believe." Why should it be so hard to do the same thing with Santa?

And if it *is* hard—if the Santa myth is so fragile that a six-year-old classmate's comment can undermine it—then why do we all cling to it this way?

I'm not sure. There's no dodging the fact that Santa's not a very fully developed deity. He hasn't been around for that long. Despite all the legends about Saint Nicholas bringing those three pickled boys back to life, it was Clement C. Moore's *A Visit From St. Nicholas*, published in 1822, that brought Santa alive in the American imagination. He only comes alive once a year; the rest of the time, we stash him up

at the North Pole in the same way we stash the boxes of ornaments in the attic. (If the elves are the ones who make the toys all year, what is Santa doing? He only has to work one night out of 365. He can't need *that* much rest.) Maybe it makes people nervous to have to bring him out and dust him off every year; they have to recreate him anew each time, and the resulting unease makes them try too hard.

But I think it's more likely that Santa has somehow become the repository for a lot of parental anxiety about giving presents. Here are a few of my theories:

☆ *We're afraid that the kids will be disappointed.* If Santa's the one responsible for the presents, *he's* the one who will be disappointing the children, not us.

☆ *If Santa does happen to disappoint the kids, we can conveniently place the blame on their own bad behavior.* Using Santa as a bribe unloads some child-rearing responsibility from ourselves. We're not nagging the kids; we're just reminding them that if they behave better there's something in it for them. This is unattractive for so many reasons that I don't know where to start.

☆ *Deep down, we know that presents don't really "go" with Christmas.* We also feel guilty about our obsession with gift-giving and -getting. We therefore dump even more responsibility on Santa's jolly shoulders to divert it away from ourselves. *Hey, kids, I didn't just give you that electric car! Santa did!*

Well, this isn't that big a deal; there's no sense delving too deeply into the psychology of a nonexistent being. But it will be easier for kids—and for their parents—if we're clear about why we're adding Santa Claus to the lineup of household gods. It's fine if he's there to add a little icing to the cake, or rather to add some whipped cream to an already iced cake. He shouldn't be asked to do much more than that. He shouldn't

make Christmas more stressful for parents or children, and he certainly shouldn't pose a problem if other kids don't believe in him. He's not important enough.

If I were starting over, I would tell my kids from the outset something on the order of, "There's a wonderful story about a man called Santa. They say he lives at the North Pole . . ." That way I'd be bringing him into the family more subtly than David and I in fact did, and I'd at least know it was on record that I had said Santa was just a story. It's too late for my own children, of course, but I'm going to try to persuade them to introduce Santa to *their* children that way. (I bet they won't, though.)

Lightening up on Santa will also help children once they're old enough to start wondering about him. It often makes kids uneasy when they start to suspect the truth. "I have a theory," my friend Beth's daughter once told her, "and I'm going to test it by not letting you see my Christmas list this year." That was more calm and rational than many kids who get frantic over the idea that Santa may not be real.

When Laura was three, she asked David if Santa really brings everything you ask for—because if so, she wanted to add "fake charcoal and a whip" to her list, which already included a Fisher-Price doctor's kit and a pet rat. (She got the rat and the doctor's kit. Shortly thereafter we had fourteen rats, no thanks to the doctor's kit.) Then Laura said to her father— whom my kids have always chosen to call by his first name— "Dave, you know Santa is not real." She took it back immediately, but still, the germ was there. John, three and a half years younger, was always a more intense believer. In third grade, John called me into his room when he was supposed to be asleep. "You have to tell me whether Santa is real *right now*," he said tearfully.

This was a poser. The previous year, we had already used "What do you think? You're the one who gets the presents." So that was out. The fact that John was so worked up showed that he suspected the truth—but it didn't necessarily mean he wanted the truth or that hearing the truth at night was the right time for it. At the same time, saying "We'll talk about it in the morning" would have given the topic too much weight. Remember: Santa's meant to be fun. He's not supposed to be a big opportunity for a child's personal growth.

So I kind of shrugged and said, "Well, I don't know if Santa is real or not, but I believe in him." Thinking frantically, *It's not really a lie because I do believe in the* spirit *of Santa.*

John sat up in bed. "You *do?*"

"Sure!"

"Oh, thank you," said John. "That was just what I needed to hear." And he snuggled back down again.

I still don't know exactly why this worked. John insists that I "swore to God" that I believed in Santa, which isn't what I remember. Though again, if I *did* say it, it wasn't a lie, right? What I think is that John welcomed an answer that let him keep pretending for one more year.

Try to keep things light when kids ask you about Santa. Don't turn his nonexistence into A Fact Of Life. Don't try to dodge the topic by veering off toward the *spirit* of Santa Claus being real; that means nothing and won't console your child a bit. But don't try to force him down the child's throat, either. If a kid is ready to stop believing, there's nothing you can do about it—and you'll look ridiculous if you keep trying to keep Santa alive.

On the other hand, saying that *you* believe in Santa lets you off the hook in several ways. It's an easier story to stick to than "Uh-HUH, Santa is SO real." As we've seen with John, it can be reassuring to a child who's not ready to give up believing. And a child who *is* ready to shed Santa will have one of two possible reactions. Either she'll assume you're speaking symbolically, or she'll think you're a big naïve dope compared to her. Surely you're already used to that?

If you keep Santa low-key enough, your kids are likely just to stop talking about him once they stop believing in him. This is a sign that Santa's made a gentle, painless exit.

Santa Claus vs. Jesus

As with many children, my kids became much more interested in the Jesus-in-the-manger story once they were old enough to be in the Christmas pageant at Sunday School. I directed this for a couple of years, and it was known for its iconoclasm. One year, a four-year-old girl named Liza who was supposed to be one of the shepherds insisted on wearing her Halloween costume instead—so that year, baby Jesus was visited by four shepherds and a pirate. Another year, I had a discussion with a preschooler named Clai about why he couldn't carry a battery-operated candle, as one of the angels was doing. (The angel's parents had unwisely let her bring it with her, so I couldn't take it away. She kept picking her nose with it during the pageant. She was the kind of girl who only showed up for the pageant and never came to Sunday School.) I said that angels carried candles in pageants, not shepherds. Clai countered, "I was just at a pageant where all the shepherds *did* carry candles." He cheered himself up by deciding that he would be King of the Shepherds.

When my daughter, Laura, started appearing in these Sunday School pageants, Santa and Jesus began to vie for her attention every Christmas. The pageant cos-

---

Give Her a Dolly That Laughs and Cries

Our three daughters were all, in their turn, Mary in the annual church pageant. (Eventually, we produced a Joseph as well.) Inspired by the pageant, our two-and-a-half-year-old daughter named one of her dolls Jesus. Because it was her favorite, our little daughter wanted it with her much of the time. When she couldn't find it, she'd run through the house like a Holy Roller shouting, "My Jesus! My Jesus!"—J. H.

tumes were of particular religious interest to her, and she decided that "Jesus had long pants, a royal coat, shoes made of wood, and long, straight socks." I'm not going to point out that this was the same year most of Laura's friends (not Laura, though) became interested in Barbies—but giving Jesus a wardrobe does show that he was becoming more important to her.

People who wonder how to keep Santa from becoming more important to their children than Jesus are crazy. There's so much more texture to the Jesus story, and so much more for kids to think about! A baby who is also somehow a King is a pretty good fit with most children's fantasies. (When the five-year-old nephew of a friend of mine got a Nativity set for Christmas, he screamed out, "Baby Jesus is the coolest guy ever!") Then there are all the animals, and if you want to elaborate on them you can pass along the tradition that animals can speak at midnight on Christmas Eve. And then there are the Wise Men, with their fascinatingly weird gifts—especially myrrh, with its bitter perfume that breathes a life of gathering gloom.

And the stuff about the stable, and the idea that Mary is somehow very special in a way grown-ups refuse to explain. "What's a virgin?" the daughter of friends of ours asked for three Christmases in a row. (They pretended not to hear.) And the weirdly technical line in the carol: "Lo, He abhors not the Virgin's womb." And then, if you skip ahead a few pages in your children's Bible . . . why, what's *this* picture where King Herod is killing all those babies?

Elves making dollies have nothing on King Herod.

Still, in a Christmas-celebrating household where church is important, you should do what you can to bring the Nativity story to the forefront of your December activities.

You already know about Advent wreaths, right? They're round (that's where the "wreath" part comes in), with places for four candles. You can easily find them in religious-supply stores; if you're not the kind of person who frequents those, you can also easily find them in craft stores, and if you are the kind of person who likes crafts, you can easily make your own wreath. You put candles in each holder, and each Sunday of Advent, you light one more candle. Traditionally, three of the candles are purple and one—which you light on the third Sunday of Advent—is pink. That's for Rose Sunday, when the solemnity of Advent is supposed to lighten up a bit. If I had been in charge of the colors, I would have made Rose Sunday the *last* Sunday of Advent. Shouldn't things be lightening up the *closer* we get to Christmas? But I'm sure my liturgical forebears had some kind of reason I'm not deep enough to understand. Anyway, lighting the Advent wreath for Sunday supper is a good time to "religious up" the week to come.

If you have a doll bed or cradle, you can decorate it for the "arrival" of Baby Jesus: Tie bells on it, wrap the bedposts in gold ribbons, wrap empty matchboxes to look like tiny presents and stack them for Jesus' arrival. This is an old Neapolitan custom—there is a charming Neapolitan creche at the Metropolitan Museum of Art—and we always put a decorated doll bed in one of our windows. An American Girl bed would be just the right size. Those spoiled little Samanthas and Kirstens can do without their beds for a few weeks.

I'm sure that you know about Advent calendars, with a little door that you open each day until Christmas Eve. I just want to mention two things about them.

First, it's important to keep them out of a very small child's reach: Opening those little doors is often irresistible for preschoolers, and they feel terrible when they do it. When she was three, Laura came to us in tears because she'd pried open the very last door on her calendar, the one meant for Christmas Day. We consoled her and taped the doors shut. That very afternoon, Laura went to play at her friend Emily's house and saw that the doors of Emily's Advent calendar had also had to be taped shut. That cheered Laura up.

Second, *save* Advent calendars! There's no reason they can't be used again, or used simply as decorations.

Who Laughs This Way: "Ho. Ho. Ho"?

Our three little boys, aged eight, seven, and four, believed devoutly in Santa Claus for perhaps longer than any of their friends. That was because of the ritual we had on Christmas Eve. As sugarplums danced in the boys' heads upstairs, their dad would always have a late-night snack of crackers and milk while filling the stockings. He would leave the crumbs and empty milk glass on the hearth as further evidence that Santa had been there.

But one Christmas Eve, Dad forgot himself completely and substituted pretzels and beer for Santa's snack. And that year, on Christmas morning, Santa sadly became a myth forever in our house. Because our little boys knew that Santa liked crackers and milk, not pretzels and beer—only dads liked that kind of stuff.—J. L.

If you don't already own a Nativity scene, it would be a good idea to buy or make one while your children are little. I know this may sound impossibly pious, but I promise you that kids really do like setting up Nativity scenes—and there is nothing like actually handling the figures to help the Christmas story become real to them. (They also like making their own Nativity figures out of salt dough, homemade Play-doh, or beeswax, and then you have something you can use and add to each year.) When I was young, I was powerfully impressed by a friend whose family had a large wooden creche scene that they moved gradually through their house as Christmas came closer. Mary and Joseph and the donkey moved toward the living room from one direction; the three Wise Men moved from another direction; and the shepherds, sheep, and manger were already waiting in the living room. On Christmas Eve, when all the figures had arrived, the Jesus figure was finally put into the manger.

Of course putting Jesus into the manger should come after hanging the stockings and doing any other Santa stuff, to weight the evening in the right religious direction. And, by the way, if you put out food for Santa, please put it in a different part of the room. Don't leave Santa's food anywhere near that doll bed you decorated for Baby Jesus. I can't answer for the consequences if Santa and Jesus were both to arrive at the same time. Another good reason for keeping them separate!

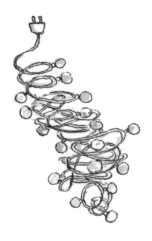

6

It's All My Husband's Fault

a special missive for wives

O then bespoke Mary, so meek and so mild,
Pluck me one cherry, Joseph, for I am with child.
O then bespoke Joseph with words most unkind,
Let him pluck thee a cherry that brought thee with child.
—"THE CHERRY-TREE CAROL"

If you ask me, Joseph had a heavy load. He had a lot of fetching and carrying—what with that donkey, and Bethlehem, and the flight into Egypt—for someone else's baby. And then, later, when Jesus reached the Terrible Twos (and you *know* someone like Jesus would have gone through every behavior stage much more intensely than most children), it must have been hard for Joseph to know how to discipline him. He couldn't be all that strict knowing that Jesus' real father was looking over his shoulder, and he could never use the threat "When your father gets home, He'll deal with this." Probably he left it all up to Mary.

I can just imagine Joseph grumbling to himself as he tried to get the stable ready on that first Christmas Eve, wishing he'd picked a wife who didn't get so *involved* in the holidays.

And thereby setting the pattern for many future husbands on many future Christmases.

The traditional Christmas fight

"I have never hated you as much as I do at this moment," a relative of mine hissed at her husband one memorable Christmas morning. It wasn't me, I swear! But I'm sure she spoke for many wives at this blessed season. And I'm equally sure that her hapless husband—who was bearing the brunt of all this fury because he'd had the audacity to take a walk instead of washing the breakfast dishes while his wife and kids were at church—agreed with her, in reverse. Christmas has *such* a way of bringing out the best in a relationship!

One of the worst fights David and I have ever had was on Christmas Eve, or rather Christmas morning between 2:00 and 4:00 A.M. This was the first year we'd spent Christmas in our new house, and we had only lived there full-time for a couple of months. The living room was full of unpacked boxes, which were to remain there for the next several years, there was bare Sheetrock everywhere, and Laura was eighteen months old. At Christmas dinner that year, she took a bite out of one of our crystal wineglasses, but that's another story. Anyway, David's parents and his younger brother were visiting us, and all Christmas Eve Day the men worked on some remodeling project in the basement. The project seemed mostly to involve sawing. A massive, droning, endless *ZZZZzzzzZZZZzzzz* filled the first floor all day long. Occasionally the sawing was punctuated by hammering and drilling, but mostly not. Mostly David's mom and I attempted to get ready for Christmas while braying at each other above the noise.

It kind of frays your nerves to try and build up a Christmas-y feeling while a saw is screeching all around you. By dinnertime, I was seething. As I dressed to go to Midnight Mass with David's mother, I believe I may have let slip from clenched teeth a few mildly reasonable words about how SOME GUYS

AROUND HERE had better PITCH IN AND DO THEIR DAMN SHARE to get ready for Christmas. Then my mother-in-law and I went off to church in the rain.

We got home at 1:00 A.M. to a peaceful, quiet house. The presents were set out under the tree, the kitchen was cleaned up, and everyone was asleep. I was proud of myself. I had communicated my needs, and my strict words had been effective! I did a few more things, tiptoed upstairs and quietly went into the bedroom—to find that David was wide awake, furious, and threateningly brandishing that hated saw toward me in the dark. Well, the part about the saw may be a trick of my memory, but the wide-awake-and-furious part was certainly true.

There followed a deeply venomous argument, all conducted in hissed, spitty whispers so that David's parents wouldn't hear us in the guest room. I won't go into specifics here, but the gist was as follows:

David: Why did you have to be such a nag tonight when we'd already been helping all day?

Me: *What* help? You call making all that noise in the cellar "help"? We couldn't even play Christmas carols, you guys were so loud! How's that supposed to be Christmas-y?

David: I don't think there's any better way to celebrate Christmas than by doing something for the house and making something for the people I love!

Me: Families are supposed to be together for Christmas, not some of them making noise in the basement while the others try to get things done on their first Christmas in their new house!

David: Oh, yeah, as if you and my mom would really have liked the three guys being upstairs in the kitchen while you were running around! We would just have been in the way!

Me: I have never hated you as much as I do at this moment!

It went on like this until 4:00 A.M., when I don't even remember what happened. Maybe we called a truce; more likely we stayed mad and just lay there, tensely pretending to be asleep. In any case, Laura woke up at her usual 6:00 A.M., bright and eager for the day to begin.

Twenty years, later, I feel so very, very right about my side of the story that I can hardly bear to admit that David believes with equal fervor in *his* side. When he first heard about this book he said that I "could" use the story about the fight—as if I hadn't had it bronzed years ago to preserve it for just this occasion. I bet that without half-trying, we could start the same fight and have it blaze up just as brightly now.

Or what about the landfill issue?

"I have just one request about the stockings," said David in the Year of Our Lord, 2003. "This year, please don't give us any landfill."

I had never hated him as much as I did at that moment. *Landfill.* That would be the stocking stuffers, which are one of my favorite things to choose for the kids. Things like—oh, I don't know—soap that looks like quartz, and nailbrushes that look like penguins, and whoopie cushions that look like whoopie cushions. Whoopie cushion design hasn't evolved much in the past fifty years.

Okay, so stocking stuffers aren't exactly useful! But they're one of the children's favorite parts of Christmas. A few years ago, I tried making the stockings more sensible, and the kids— well, they didn't complain, but they Mentioned It.

On the other hand, David has a point. Months after Christmas, the stocking stuffers always turn up under a bed somewhere, decanted into a shopping bag and forgotten about. It's not as though my daughter's going to take that stuff back to college with her, and my son doesn't plan to keep the hilarious wind-up "chattering teeth" in his locker. Usually the candy in our stockings is the only thing that gets touched—and even so, I still have a Santa lollipop sitting next to my computer from Christmas 2002.

The Landfill vs. Stocking Stuffer debate pretty much sums up a common—um, let's call it a "situation" (to keep things neutral)—in many traditional Christmastime households. Landfill vs. Stocking Stuffers could translate into "Sensible vs.

Over the River and Through the Woods

We don't fit the traditional pattern, since my wife hates Christmas. I do the tree-trimming with our daughter, and almost everything else regarding Christmas decorations, plans, etc. My wife Susan's family had no significant Christmas tradition, except for an enormous fight every Christmas morning. (The biggest fight ever concerned the correct spelling of "Earhart" after my wife, the youngest of five kids, tried to name her new Patty Play Pal doll "Amelia.")

Our family, on the other hand, always did up Christmas big. We always went back home for Christmas, and so did all my siblings and their families. Every single Christmas throughout my twenties, thirties, and forties—until the eighth year of my marriage to Susan—every single Benson and every single Benson spouse showed up at my parents' house for Christmas. I actually loved it; the problem was that Susan hated, hated, hated it—four or five days cooped up at my parents'—our main travel expense of the year—to celebrate a holiday that gave her the willies anyway, in a teetotaling household. Plus we always did exactly the same thing each year, and everything had to be done en masse—movies, church, trips to the zoo, the annual pointless pilgrimage to see the lights in the next city. Only once or twice did Susan and I get off by ourselves to do something. Finally she put her foot down, and when she did my brother's wife confessed that she too had hated it all those years but had been too intimidated to put her foot down. It was a big sore spot in our marriage; years later, it's still a big sore spot.—F. B.

Frivolous." Or "Thrifty vs. Spendthrift." Or "Boring vs. Fun." Or "Bored and Left Out vs. Manic and Way Over-Involved." Or husbands vs. wives.

Our Christmas "roles"

In his book *The Intentional Family: Simple Rituals to Strengthen Family Ties*, family therapist William J. Doherty came up with an inspired description of most husbands and wives at this blessed season. I wish I could steal his account and put it into my own words, but unfortunately, it's already been perfectly expressed. As Doherty explains:

> Like any complex enterprise, Christmas requires a competent executive director, whom I call the Family Christmas Coordinator, the one person in most families who is in charge of putting the whole production together. Again, traditionally, this role belongs to the wife/mother of the family. . . . For many women, Christmas is like a major athletic event, and August is not too soon to begin working out and making advance game plans.
>
> Since family roles generally come in pairs, the Christmas Coordinator in this holiday dance is paired with the "Christmas Abstainer," usually a man (in heterosexual couples), who stays aloof from the demands of the season while being vaguely aware that the Coordinator is getting hard to live with. A predictable series of interactions between the Coordinator and the Abstainer begin soon after Thanksgiving. As the Coordinator becomes more obsessed with holiday preparations, the Abstainer becomes more detached and irritable, while the children for their part are becoming more excited and demanding.
>
> *   *   *
>
> By Christmas Eve, the melodrama is underway, and usually is not being played according to the Coordinator's script. She is exhausted, worried about the outcome, annoyed by fault-finding relatives, and still hoping that the "pageant" will come

off as promised. For months, she has shouldered the entire burden of Christmas, an unsung martyr who is growing tired of her cross. At last, appealing for help to the Abstainer, she breaks down in frustration, only to hear him accuse her of overreacting, getting worked up over nothing, flying off the handle.

When I described the Coordinator-Abstainer thing to my husband, he said knowingly, "Sound familiar?" *Well, duh, David! That's why I mentioned it! I was trying to meet you halfway!* I had never hated him as much as I hated him at that moment.

But it really fits all too well, and it has ever since our first Christmas together.

The first year that David and I were married, we stayed in our apartment alone at Christmas because he couldn't get enough time off work to travel. Since our younger siblings all still lived at home, neither set of parents could visit us. I was sad about this, having assumed we'd spend Christmas with my parents, but I cheered up when I realized that being on our own would give me a great chance to try out all of my family's traditions and jettison all of David's. How could he care?, I reasoned. My family's Christmases were so richly perfect, and his family's were probably so skimpy and pathetic! Why, he should be grateful to me for giving him the chance to spend a really *nice* holiday instead of what he'd been used to.

I don't know that you'll be surprised to hear that it didn't quite work out that way. We had friends over for Christmas dinner. This seemed like a huge concession to me, since my nuclear family had never fraternized with outsiders on Christmas Day. I roasted my first goose with much angst. After dinner, David played loud music on the stereo—among other crimes. I don't know how I had been expecting to entertain our friends. Did I think we were all going to read *A Child's Christmas in Wales* aloud? Whatever I had imagined, loud non-Christmas music was not part of it. I had never hated David as much as I did at that moment.

And with no reason! You'd think I might have said, "Well, we *are* all in our early twenties, and I suppose that entertaining our friends in an age-appropriate way is as Christmas-y as anything else." (Yes, I always speak precisely as pompously as that.) But no. I'm sure I just sat there and glowered, because although David was celebrating Christmas, *he wasn't celebrating it my way*.

In the same way that brides assume they're the important ones on their wedding day—and the groom is nothing but some prop in a tux whose job is to stand admiringly out of the way—wives often assume that they're the ones whose vision of Christmas should prevail. No matter that their husbands come from homes where, presumably, Christmas was celebrated just as richly as in the wives' families. (Husbands are, after all, the sons of wives.) As far as the wife is concerned, her husband's family might as well have handed out Christmas presents in the Wal-Mart parking lot and then gone to T. G. I. Friday's for a beer. It's not too surprising, therefore, that when husbands begin to realize that they're *still* nothing but a prop whose job is to stand admiringly out of the way, they lose interest in the Christmas factory their wives are directing.

Of course husbands do have other Christmas chores besides

Tiny Tots With Their Eyes All Aglow...

Every Christmas my mother worried that perhaps she'd inadvertently shortchanged one of us. After we had opened all our presents, she would try to make us—especially herself—feel better by saying something like this:

"Well, Patty got the most presents, Sarah Jane got the best presents, and Richie got the most expensive presents."

Meanwhile, my father, mentally calculating how much had been spent, would mutter, "Jesus Christ, Janice, we're Jewish!"—P. M.

standing around cheering their wives on. And they're such festive chores, aren't they! Here are some of the tasks wives traditionally outsource at Christmas:

☆ *Putting the tree into its stand.* Delightful! Even if you have one of those Ultimate Swivel Action It Can't Possibly End Up Crooked stands, the job is not fit for humans. One year, when we'd just finished decorating the tree, it suddenly began to topple over *again.* I rushed to hold it upright while David rushed underneath it—all the ornaments falling off and bopping down onto his back—and tried to fumble it back into the stand. Laura helpfully picked up a fallen Christmas-tree ornament and stuck the hook through my ear as if it were an earring. Oh, how we all laughed, except David. He was still crouched under seventy pounds of branches. "What's funny?" he grunted.

☆ *Putting the lights on the tree.* Daddy pulls the hideous tangle out of the box, then carefully uncoils and spreads the strings of lights out on the living room floor to check the bulbs. How can anyone step on the lights? Everyone sees what he's doing; it's the only job going on in the living room at that point. Nevertheless, there is a continuous crunching sound as family member after family member accidentally treads on one of the strings. Dad gets increasingly grumpy about this, especially when he, too, walks on one of the strings. When all the glass is swept up, he starts putting on the lights. The tree is still so nice and fresh that he has to armwrestle each branch into submission. After hours of having the branches win, Daddy plugs in the tree and stands back to admire his handiwork. Only then does he realize that a defective bulb has turned off half the lights on the tree. Is he willing to check the bulbs again, one by one? No, but Mommy's and the kids' heartfelt cries of sorrow force him into it. Ninety minutes later the bulb is isolated and replaced. Long before that, the rest of the family has wandered away.

✰ *Stuffing the torn-off wrapping paper into black plastic garbage bags on Christmas morning.* Can Daddy get all the paper into three bags, or will he need a fourth? It's one of the mysteries of Christmas!

✰ *Taking the tree outside after the festivities are over.* Now the tree is brown and skeletal, of course, and you can hear the needles crackle as they shower to the floor. "Don't get the needles all over the place," suggests Mommy.

And, of course, worrying about the money.

The money! The money!

Oh, dear. I *so* much don't want to talk about this one. Even typing the words *money* and *worrying* in the same sentence makes my stomach feel all trembly.

I guess I have to at least mention it, though. Money is one of the biggest Christmas problems there is, and during December in my house it's always looming around the corner like an evil gas.

I wish I were a *Little Women* "We don't need a lot of money to have a good Christmas" type. Alas, I'm more of a Scarlett O'Hara "We need more money than there is in the world to have a good Christmas, and even then it's not enough" type. (I have Scarlett's seventeen-inch waist, too!) No matter how much I repeat all the Christmas/money truisms to myself—*You can't buy the Christmas Spirit! Show the kids that money is meaningless by making their presents this year! Jesus would rather have you empty your wallet into that Salvation Army bucket than do what you plan to do with it, which is to buy wired ribbon at the craft store!*— what I'm really thinking is, "A few hundred more dollars, and I could stop worrying about this."

My friend Tommy says, "We actively maintain a 'load-sharing' arrangement at my house. I'm the 'load,' and I actively share the contents of my wallet with my wife. Works for us!" I don't know whether to hope he's telling the truth, because then he'd be an example I could hold up for David. Or maybe I should hope he's exaggerating, because then I'd feel as though all couples get tense about money at Christmas, not just David and me.

Obviously the latter case is the likelier one. And equally obviously, this is the kind of problem that can't be resolved without, you know, *communicating* and stuff. Unfortunately, I don't like to communicate about money. I like to charge a reasonable amount on David's Visa card, and then charge a secret, *un*reasonable amount on my own Visa card, racking up a frightening total that I can't possibly pay off. Then I like to curse myself and worry for months at a time, while praying that I get some kind of windfall check that will magically pay off the whole total. Then I like to have that not happen, so that the following Christmas my balance can become even more unmanageable. And I like to have this happen year after year with no hope of resolution.

Since I like all this so much, it pains me to confess that this past Christmas, as

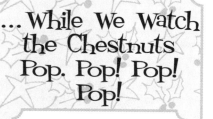

... While We Watch the Chestnuts Pop. Pop! Pop! Pop!

The last-minute shopping was finished and my parents had hidden the presents in the back of our old Subaru station wagon, which was out in the driveway. Suddenly we noticed that the car was on fire. Just about the time the fireman arrived, the real fireworks began: Dad's loaded handgun began firing inside the car. Needless to say, no one could approach the vehicle. We never found out what had caused the fire.
—M. S.

an experiment for this book, I suggested to David that we actually set a budget the way couples in books always do.

"It seems so arbitrary to do that. Why don't you just be sure not to spend too much?" David asked.

But I said I thought it would be more helpful to know what "too much" meant, and that a budget would help fend off my annual Christmas Eve Dread. This phenomenon occurs at 9:45 P.M., just before I leave for church, when David and I lay out all the presents we've bought for the kids—and suddenly what I've built up in my mind as a Taj Mahal of gifts sweeps up into a tiny pile of rubble. David says, "Are there any other presents somewhere else in the house?" and I think desperately, *If only I'd spent more!*

I'll probably always feel that way at the last minute; it's a holiday neurosis, part of thinking I've flunked Christmas. But at least when a budget is in place, you *know* you shouldn't have spent more. You also know you've done the best you can within a set of guidelines, which is much more comfortable than feeling as if you've been sneaking around trying to smuggle more presents into the house.

Budgeting does require that you talk right out loud about a scary topic, and maybe even negotiate. A dreadful plight, but there's a good chance you'll feel better once it's all out in the open, whereas feeling furtive ends up being quite uncomfortable in the long run. True, I gave my father a StickyPad from Despair, Inc. last Christmas that was printed with the saying, "Hard work often pays off after time, but laziness always pays off now." But that's only true for things like cleaning up your desk—not for Big Important Talks About A Budget.

In any case, David and I agreed on a figure (eighteen cents per person), and I can't say the kids seemed deprived last Christmas. So far, they show no signs of lingering bitterness, either. Maybe we've solved the problem and can move on to fighting about something else at Christmas—like that time he and his father and brother did all that *sawing*.

7

The Other Holiday Visitors

coping with relatives at christmas

Supposing, let us say, your wife's folks who live up in East Russet, Vermont, write and ask you to come up and bring the children for a good old-fashioned Christmas, "while we are all still together," they add cheerily with their flair for putting everybody in good humor.

—ROBERT BENCHLEY, *A GOOD OLD-FASHIONED CHRISTMAS*

You're not going to believe this. One Christmas my parents were visiting, and they actually . . .

Yeah, right. Did you really think I was going to use this chapter to spill my guts about my *own* family? Oh, no no no no no. My family's going to be reading this! Anyway, my family is perfect.

But you may not be so lucky.

"I'm looking forward to seeing my parents this Christmas," a college acquaintance of mine said many years ago, "Because I'm really going to have it out with them."

For some reason, visiting relatives have a way of becoming even more like themselves at Christmas. And I don't mean that as a compliment. As you surely know by now—and from your own experience, not just from my going on about it—

Christmas makes everyone needy. A Christmas holiday spent with a large number of relatives can be reminiscent of one of those experiments where they cram more and more rats into a very small space. The rats get more and more short-tempered and aggressive. And rats don't have all that Christmas expectation hanging over their heads, and they don't get angry at themselves if they eat too much. And I've owned plenty of pet rats in my time, so I know this much is true: They don't have family dynamics to screw up.

Given that a kindly giant scientist isn't about to pick up half your family and move them into a different house if things get too tense at Christmas, you may need to come up with a few coping strategies.

Expect the worse—in a nice way

Of course there are things you can't always prepare for. Once, my brother-in-law jauntily said to Laura, who was then four, "So, Laura! Do you still believe in Santa?" I can't remember what happened after that, because my brain froze up in panic.

But you can predict a few things.

My friend Richard often spends Christmas with his entire extended family. He knows he can expect his mother to interrupt everyone, all the time. "She installs herself in a chair, and whenever she happens to think of something to say or ask, she immediately barks it out loudly, with no thought as to where anyone else in the house might be or what they might be doing."

One of Richard's sisters is another problematic visitor. "She wants to make every second of the visit 'count' at a deep emotional level. She likes to engage in deep, meaningful conversation twenty-four hours a day and will always be there at your side, like a hungry dog, longing to relate emotionally. One thing I've noticed is that she always turns her body to face you for full-frontal conversation, even if you're seated side by side in the car or at table. During one Christmas visit, after facing me head-on for an hour when we were sitting on the sofa watching a football game—I, of course, was facing the TV, avoiding her—she commented, 'You know what? You have a big nose.'"

Most holiday visits last for at least a couple of days, and it's best to know up front that you have no chance of rehabilitating people like this. Interrupters you can sometimes ignore, although what I like to do is blare out "*I'M* TALKING" and then, in the brief instant that they're startled into silence, go right on talking. This worked when I was a Sunday School teacher, and it sometimes works with adults as well.

People who like meaningful dialogue are more difficult, especially if you're trying to make a *bûche de Noël* or something. My aunt Jeanette liked to come into the kitchen, plant herself an inch away from me while I was cooking, and say like, "So, Ann. What do you think about the situation in the Middle East?" This was the same aunt who made a special point, on my mother's sixth birthday, of showing her the *Life* magazine photo of a sobbing Shanghai baby in the bombing of Nanking. "She needs to learn about things like this," Aunt Jeannette said.

I loathe deep conversation, but fortunately the kind of people who love it are easy to distract. All you have to do is ask them a few questions about everyone's favorite topic— themselves—and they'll be off and running. In the case of the Middle East question, I should have said, "I'm not sure what to think. What do *you* think?" (Instead, I made clipped one-word replies while angrily continuing to stir with my back turned to my poor aunt, who later said, "I feel as if we haven't really talked during this visit.") You can switch off your brain and continue with whatever you're doing, interjecting another question from time to time. You'll get points for being a great listener, and you won't get trapped into making nonsensical remarks about the Middle East that Aunt Jeannette will later attribute to you at the dinner table.

Be ready for Christmas spirits

You can be absolutely sure that a relative who drinks too much *will* want to drink too much at your house.

Don't sit around hoping that this time it won't happen. Decide what you're going to do. Are you going to "solve" the problem by keeping a very limited amount of alcohol available? That's the route I always like to take—and it's a no-brainer if teenagers are in the house—but it doesn't exactly simplify things. And you can't keep a drunk from going to the liquor store and bringing stuff back. Still, if someone's drinking makes you uncomfortable, you don't need to have any alcohol around, and you don't need to offer any. You're allowed to make the rules in your own house! And at least this way, when the drinker inevitably overdoes it, you will know that you didn't contribute to the problem.

A friend of mine who is wise in these matters adds:

"On the other hand, you shouldn't feel any obligation to deny him liquor because you don't want to contribute to his problem. His problem has nothing to do with you, and whether you serve him or not will have no effect on his being an alcoholic or getting sober. Sometimes the most spiritual thing you can do is give a drunk a drink.

"In the end, you are probably screwed either way. If you set limits, it may require confronting him,

In the Bleak Midwinter...

A friend of mine spent Christmas with her hippie brother and said it was a total nightmare. He and his wife made a huge point—and made it repeatedly—of saying that they had bought toilet paper especially for the coddled city folk.—B. K.

throwing him out, or otherwise causing a scene—because odds are he will find a way to get drunk anyway. If you don't set limits, and you are offended by his behavior when he's drunk, then you will probably end up feeling uncomfortable for that reason.

"Whichever you do, though, try to keep a little Christmas spirit in your heart—even if you decide to be strict with him. Remember, he's not bad, he's sick. But that doesn't give him the right to ruin your Christmas."

Just so.

It's hard, I know. A friend of mine forbade her father to drink in front of her children when her parents visited at Christmas. He managed to stay on the wagon during the visit. Then, when he returned home, he got so drunk that he fell down the stairs and broke his hip. Her mother's first words: "If you had let Daddy drink at your house, this wouldn't have happened."

Beating bossiness

Bossy relatives do not generally become less bossy in large gatherings. They typically become *more* so. Sometimes this is done in a very indirect, nice way—so subtly that the victims don't even realize what's going on but find themselves getting into a worse and worse mood for reasons they can't quite grasp. This is my preferred tactic when I'm feeling bossy. "That's an interesting way of washing the dishes," I'll remark. "I don't remember ever seeing it done that way before." Or, "You know, if you chill the beaters first"—this as someone is halfway through whipping a pint of cream—"it will go much faster."

Sometimes the bossing around is more overt than mine. My friend Valerie's mom is famously unstoppable. While visiting her son and daughter-in-law one Christmas, she took it upon herself to reorganize their spice cupboard. Glenn, the son, opened the cabinet and found that nothing looked familiar. "Where's the pepper?" he asked. His mother pointed. "It's alphabetical," she said, "the way it *should* be." And it was: She had lined everything up in alphabetical order.

Then there's my friend Patty's grandmother, who once remarked, "If I have to eat broccoli that's cooked like this, I can't go on living."

Judith Martin, a.k.a. Miss Manners, theorizes that the best way to deal with bossy relatives is to ask them nonstop questions about how to do everything. You can also pretend you think they're giving good advice, but then quietly go on doing everything your own way.

But most important, in all cases where people are difficult: *Instead of praying that someone will not behave badly, assume she will, and be ready for it.* Then, when the bad behavior slithers out from under its rock, you'll think, "Ah, yes. Here it is," rather than "I can't believe you did that *again*! Aren't you *ever* going to change?" This will reduce your tension considerably.

You can also take this attitude several steps further by playing The Family Game—the game that turns annoying relatives into gold.

The Family Game is evil, dangerous fun that requires family members who you completely trust. It's based on the game "Boss," which I first read about in the *Wall Street Journal*. There's a video game with the same name, but that's something else. In *this* "Boss," the office workers who are playing list all the most predictable things their boss says. You know—stuff like "We're a team" or "I welcome your input." They divide the sayings evenly among themselves and then wait. Whenever the boss utters one of the predictable sayings during a speech or at a meeting, the worker who "owns" the saying gets a point. This means that the staff actually begins to look forward to the boss's saying the things that usually drive them crazy.

Think how useful this game would be in large family gatherings! I wish my own family had played it when our aunt Gail was still alive. Back in the days when Gail was still drinking (she got sober at eighty and never looked back, I'm proud to say), you could count on her to tell you several times an hour that she'd had "one and a half years at dramatic school." Over the course of the evening, this would become "one-half years dramat'c shchool." We all used to sit tensely, pre-flinching, dreading the next time she'd utter the line again. But if we could have gotten *points* every time she said it—or every time my grandpa Crosby told us he'd had "cholera morbus" as a little boy, or every time Grandma Joyce said "So! Well!" or "How may I be of assistance?"—we would have waited with breathless anticipation.

We might even have figured out ways to get more points for our side. "Is there anything you'd like to learn about, Aunt

Our Cheeks Are Nice and Rosy, and Comfy-Cosy Are We...

I was only a kid, but I remember this Christmas Day clearly. Mom, Dad, my brother, and I were at Dad's parents' house for the usual festivities. I think it all started with the eggnog. By 10:00 A.M., Mom was sloshed. I had never seen anyone behaving in this manner, especially not my very proper mother. It was all fun and games until my mom handed my aunt a platter of food and said, "Take this to the table, you dumb Polack."

Mom was not aware of having said anything inappropriate, but there was no more laughing. For the rest of the day, she lay on the bathroom floor. She locked herself in and would not open the door for anyone. All you could hear was the constant scraping from inside as she used the old-fashioned iron doorstop to "iron" the floor.—J. S.

Elsie?" ("I wish I knew something about computers. I'd like to take a computer course at the high school sometime." *Score!*) "How would you describe the experience, Aunt Meggie?" ("It was very special." *Score!*)

Children! Go where I send thee!

Let's not forget that adults aren't the only houseguests who can behave badly at Christmas. Children, especially those who are not one's own, can be just as bad.

Sometimes they're too little to blame. "Don't you have any CDs she can break?" a friend of mine once said when her eighteen-month-old was busily prying open all my CD boxes and shaking the discs to the ground. I would have thought that finding another activity for the baby would be the obvious choice for my friend, though I do remember the days when a baby has whomped you so badly that you're incapable of doing anything besides listlessly watching her destroy things. So we moved into the kitchen instead, where I didn't mind having the baby take out all the pots and pans.

But sometimes children are old enough that *someone* should be saying *something* to them, and it doesn't appear that either of their parents is going to be that someone.

Here's what I will say instead: *There is nothing you can do about it. Let it go.*

Oh, you can keep an obnoxious kid—we'll call him or her the O.K.—from breaking something, if you get there in time. You must definitely move your own children out of the way if the O.K. starts swatting them. But all you can do is deal with specific, individual problems like these. You will not be able to make the O.K. become a nice child during the visit. And there's nothing you can say or do to the O.K.'s parents that won't make things worse while you're all under the same roof.

I'm sorry. You were hoping I'd provide you with a fabulous coping strategy. Something that would make the O.K. behave while not making you look like the heavy, and something that wouldn't make the O.K.'s parents feel as if you were trying to take over their job.

I promise you: No such strategy exists. Not for a short-term situation.

When I'm with other people's misbehaving children, I always find myself thinking, "If you were *my* kids, you'd shape up." But a) That's not necessarily true, and even if it is, they wouldn't shape up by Christmas Day; b) They never *will* be my children, so it's a pointless thought to have; and c) They may not even be be-having that badly. Everyone always thinks everyone else's chil-dren are out of control—especially if those children are relatives.

Another thing to keep in mind is that adults at family gath-erings tend to ignore their kids too much. It's so tempting just to stretch out and watch reruns of *Marcus Welby, M.D.* with one's adult siblings! You sit there lazily thinking, "The cousins will all get along. That's what cousins do," and minutely dis-secting the behavior of that mean lady who lived down the street when you were little. Meanwhile, you're expecting children who may have little in common to play nicely simply because they're young and related.

When there's a gathering of children who don't know each other that well, or who are of varied ages, one or two of the adults present *must* step in and direct the child traffic. It's not Christmas-y to expect the kids to fend for themselves the whole time. Plan some activities ahead of time if possible. If you haven't done that, take the children outside to play tag, do a craft or a puzzle with them, go try on Grandma's old dresses—anything. Then, when you've done a fair share, an-other adult or two should spell you. Ideally, the whole family should do a couple of things together (eating Christmas dinner doesn't count), but when that's not possible, adults need to provide some structure for the kids.

You will soon realize that focusing your attention on enter-taining the children actually uses up less mental energy than trying to relax on the sofa, thumbing through your old yearbooks and telling yourself that the kids—whom you can clearly hear scream-

Brightly Shone the Moon That Night...

I can remember as a child that my fat uncle bent over to pick up a present from under the tree and his khakis split right up the butt—and he was commando, if you catch my drift.
—D. R. M.

ing at one another in the basement—will be fine. It's also just about the only way to help keep an obstreperous child in line. Getting a concentrated blast of interest and attention often makes obnoxious children calm down and stop picking on *your* children. And children of varying ages can often play together better if an adult is playing along with them.

Television doesn't count as entertainment, by the way. That's for when the adults have involved themselves enough with the children that they deserve some time to themselves. And if you're thinking that it's not fair to you to have to spend your holiday baby-sitting—well, it's less fair to throw the kids into a pile and see which of them can struggle to the surface intact. Who's the adult here? You'll have plenty of time for grown-up conversation when your children have moved out of the house.

By the way, a good variant of The Family Game involves amassing points for the number of times a small child repeats something. Once, during a meltdown on a long car ride, a nephew of mine began to wish for some black jellybeans, which at the time he called "jack bellabeans." He cried out, "I want my jack bellabeans!" four times from the backseat of the car, restlessly switching his legs about. His mother (my sister) and I tacitly agreed to ignore him, since the jack bellabeans were packed in a carry-on bag for the plane trip, and he was too worked up to reason with. After the fourth time he mentioned them, my sister whispered, "Let's count how many times he says it." He said it twenty-eight times.

Expect the worst about yourself (in the best possible way)

You know yourself, so you can predict how you will *react* when relatives *act*.

For example, I'm bad at letting people help me when I'm cooking. I like to focus on the cooking so much that I'd almost rather prepare a twenty-course meal alone than have my attention divided by parceling out different tasks to different people. In fact, I designed our kitchen so that during most of my prep work, my back is to everyone else in the room.

But when I have guests—especially at Christmas—this is a useless and uncharitable way to be have. No one likes to sit around a kitchen watching me work myself into a stupor. People *want* to help, and they're not going to stop offering to help no matter how many times I say, "No, no, I'm fine." Especially when I'm frantically busy and clearly not fine at all.

So when I start cooking with guests in the house, I mentally set aside all the chores that can be parceled out. (It can't be all the boring things like peeling the potatoes, either. Some of it has to be making the desserts.) And I remind myself that it's not my job to stand over whoever is helping me and point out little things the helper might do differently. If you accept help at Christmas—and you should, to increase the Christmas spirit—you have to let go and accept that everything will not be done exactly the way you'd do it if you were all by yourself.

If you know that one relative tends to bring up a topic that enrages you—oh, let me just pick an example out of the air here, one that has nothing to do with anyone in my own family, an example such as "Ann, wouldn't you agree that organic farming is pointless?"—you can have a couple of answers ready. I mean, answers besides "Shut up, you kill-y pesticide lover." Something more on the order of "Relative-who-is-not-in-my-own-family, I'm guessing we won't get anywhere with this subject."

Break up the group often

Never, never do things in a pack all day long! That is the surest path to festering irritation—at least if I'm staying at your house or you're staying at mine. Both houseguests and their hosts need big chunks of time when they can be alone or with only a couple of people.

Also, try to make sure that the adult nappers in the group get time for naps. My sister Nelie and I nap religiously. We take turns watching the kids whenever we're together so that we can each get that vital hour in the afternoon. When I think how much I hated naps as a kid—what a waste! If only I could have all that enforced naptime again now . . .

Warn your children ...

There are a lot of things to warn them about, and I'm not talking about their avoiding the F-word in front of Nana.

Small children—well, *all* children, probably—get distressed and annoyed when they see their parents acting differently from the way they usually do. When my sister Cathy and I were little we used to talk about my mother's "phone laugh," which sounded completely different from her normal laugh. It was more of a polite, social vocalization than an actual laugh, and we always picked up on it right away.

Think of all the times you act fake when there's company in the house. All the ways you try to start a conversation, or to keep it going . . . the false brightness in your voice . . . the exaggerations you make to keep things interesting (or at least I do) . . . Your children are going to notice this kind of thing, and if they're the way *my* children used to be, they're going to call you on it or disagree with you in a way that wrecks your efforts.

Trying to think of something, *anything*, to say, you tell your uncle Howard—shouting, because Uncle Howard is deaf—

"Fifi had some great news at school this week! She was picked for the lead in the play!"

Fifi scowls, looks down, and mutters, "They picked two other girls, too. We have to rotate."

"What, dear?" says Uncle Howard.

"WE HAVE TO ROTATE," bawls Fifi. This makes no sense to Uncle Howard, and why should it? By now you wish that Fifi had never been born. She, of course, is wishing the same thing about you.

When Laura and John were little, I used to remind them that grown-ups sometimes behaved differently in company, and that grown-ups sometimes felt just as shy and unnatural with one another as kids do. I asked them please not to derail a conversation by pointing it out when I said something that wasn't strictly accurate or that didn't sound like me. They could complain about it privately if they wanted, I said. And you know what? They did!

Make everyone play a couple of games

Besides The Family Game, I mean. Never forget Pictionary, the best store-bought family game ever. You probably have it in some cupboard somewhere. Dig it out right now! The only difficulty with Pictionary is that very young children simply can't play it on the same level as older kids and adults. Either they can't draw fast enough, or they don't understand the word they're given to illustrate. (What would a six-year-old make of *mud flap*?)

There are a few ways around this. One is to let the child keep picking a card until s/he gets something drawable—and give him or her two flips of the hourglass timer instead of one. Or have it be only the adults who draw, and the kids who guess what they're drawing. Or use two sets of cards—one from the adult version of the game, one from the child's version.

My friend Bill reminded me of an old parlor game that his family plays every Christmas Eve—one that's also perfect for multiple generations. It's called the Name Game, and he and his family always play it on Christmas Eve. I'll let him tell you about it.

"The Name Game is a good transition from dinner to dessert and coffee," says Bill. "It gives everyone a chance to stop eating for a while and to move around a bit. We send the younger generation upstairs, and the older generation stays downstairs. The downstairs group thinks up one name for every person upstairs and vice versa. The names get written on a piece of paper and taped to the appropriate forehead. It's a great sight gag—everyone dressed up, all sitting around a table full of candles, with names taped to their foreheads.

"We go around the table and everyone has to guess who they are by asking as few questions as possible. The only name guideline is that everyone at the dinner table has to have heard of the person. So they don't have to be famous names, they can also be names from [your own] family lore. When my nephew Hobie used to do magic acts at family reunions years ago, he used to call himself Professor Rosseforp. I had that palindrome stuck to my forehead last year, much to the delight of the rest of the table. It wasn't easy establishing the category my name belonged in.

"Also: The names are chosen more for who will be guessing them than for difficulty. This year, still smarting from the Red Sox's heartbreaking eleventh-inning American League Championship loss to the hated Yankees in October, my son Charlie had to wear the name George Steinbrenner. Uncle Richard has always loudly hated Bruce Springsteen, so one year the kids couldn't wait to put that name on him. Other names from recent years: Strom Thurmond, Marge Simpson, Patti LaBelle, Socrates, Ferris Bueller, Louis XIV, Colonel Sanders, and Eleanor Roosevelt."

I can't imagine any family not liking The Name Game, and I'm going to make sure my own family plays it next Christmas. I can't wait to see whether they give me the name Mother Teresa or Helen of Troy. It's sure to be one of those two, don't you think?

8

O, Tanenbaum!

some cranky thoughts about christmas trees

P. B. was being allowed to decorate a big tree in the garden, all by himself and with a ladder. Suddenly we heard terrible growly-squeaky noises. We rushed out to find P. B. hanging in the tree himself. "You are *not* a decoration," shouted Father Christmas.

J. R. R. TOLKIEN, *LETTERS FROM FATHER CHRISTMAS*

One of the worst demonstrations of my badness is that my husband and I put lights on our Christmas tree instead of candles. When I was growing up, ours was the only house I knew with candles on the tree, and we felt pretty smug about it. Not for us, this crass American custom of electricity! We Hodgmans did things the right way—the *European* way. (Never mind that we weren't European.) All four of us children were determined to have candles on our trees when we grew up.

I think some of us may have managed to get candles onto one or two trees when we got married, but after that our spouses prevailed. It's true that nothing is prettier than candles on a Christmas tree; it's also true that if a Christmas tree decides to catch fire, the little red fire extinguisher you keep in the kitchen won't do anything to stop it. A dried-up Christmas tree explodes if a flame touches it.

Although I guess I'd feel pretty sad if our tree exploded and the house burned down because of my purism, I still feel bad about using lights. But now that I've celebrated twenty-six Christmases since marrying, I've managed to shove that guilt under the bed. I have another Christmas-tree secret that's even guiltier. I wish we had a nice fake tree.

The fake tree debate

When I look through the really good catalogs every November and see their beautiful, pre-lit, perfectly imperfect trees, my heart fills with lust. The catalog whose trees I most covet uses three kinds of needle-tips. "Dense, round tips for fullness; two-tone hard tips for warm color; and exploded tips of pollinating branches for softness," the text explains. "We brought in trees fresh from their native forests and scrutinized their

Seven Swans A-Swimming

We enjoyed a real Christmas tree for about fifteen years. But one particular year the trees were extremely dry, and we needed to water ours more often than in years past. I must have been in a hurry one morning and didn't notice that the tree skirt was stuck in the water well. It wasn't until after supper when I went to sit down and enjoy the tree's beauty that I noticed that the hardwood floor was a different color than I had remembered. When I looked more closely, the planks were soggy and warped. It seems that the tree skirt had drawn the water out of the well and onto the floor, where it sat for eight hours. The floor was ruined.

We are now an "artificial tree" family. It's easy. It's clean. It's indestructible. And it's a good value.—T. C.

branch formations, growth patterns, and shedding habits, then sent actual needles to the manufacturer for color matching."

Exploded tips of pollinating branches! Fresh from their native forests! They *must* be worth paying hundreds of dollars for! Even the lightbulbs on the trees are more delectable than ordinary ones: They "burn brighter with deeper, richer colors." And for extra realism, the company includes a packet of fake needles to sprinkle under the tree. I suppose that if you run out, you could gather some real needles from the backyard.

Oh, I would be so, so happy if I had one of those magical trees. Except that I would hate myself for having bought it.

In Connecticut—or at least the part of it where I live—no one has a fake tree in their house. You *have* to have a real one, preferably one that you've cut down yourself, with your teeth. Even my friends Nora and Dave, who have a jillion-foot ceiling in the living room of their converted barn, cut down their own twenty-foot tree every year. (They have a special pole for putting the ornaments on the very top.)

Of course this means you get a nice fresh tree that smells great; you "help the farmers;" and if you're the outdoorsy type, it's a nice adventure to cut down your own. When our children were very young, our tradition was to go to a place where you took a hayride to a field, picked out a tree, and cut it down yourself. One year, my husband and the kids went with my friend Martha and *her* kids. What a stir that made among the other nursery-school moms!

Capering around in the frosty air was good exercise for the children, and they liked choosing the tree even though really we only pretended they were choosing it. "That's a *beautiful* one, honey!" I'd coo. "Good *choice!*" Then on we'd walk until we found something I liked better. We'd troop back to the farmhouse and drink hot chocolate while the men baled the tree and put it on our car.

This certainly seems like the most virtuous way of getting a tree. The only show-offier way would have been to find one in our own woods (which we don't have) and drag it back to the

house ourselves. Yet as the years passed, I found myself beginning to dread the ritual. It always meant walking through a lot
of mud, for one thing. Once my sister-in-law and I went by
ourselves. The tree guy handed me a bow saw and walked
away, and Mimi and I eyed each other fearfully. We did manage at last, but it wasn't our finest hour. If you've never held a
saw in your life, a spiky tree all sticky with sap isn't the place
to start.

I switched to buying a pre-cut tree. Going to a parking lot
seemed like a step down when most of my friends were still
puritanically tramping around in the woods, and as the years
of doing *that* passed, I began to dread it as well. Not that it was
hard, it just wasn't very festive.

So I started ordering a fresh tree online, and that's what
I've been doing for the past four years. You can pick the size
and type of tree you want, and it will be cut and delivered to
your door in a big box. The advantage here is that you can slide
open the end of the box and put the tree in its stand while it's
still wrapped and lying on its side; the branches aren't all
whomping around in your face.

The disadvantage is that you don't get to see the tree before
it gets to your house, and a tree that can be packed in a mailing
box tends to be rather slender. "Our tree is . . . graceful," I
told Laura the second year I'd gotten one online. "You mean
it's too skinny, like last year?" she said instantly. For those first
two years, the trees we got were miraculously scentless as
well. How can a fresh-cut tree have no smell?

If I had a nice fake tree, none of this would be happening
(except that it, too, would have no smell). I'd just get it out of
the closet and set it up. But of course, as I said, I'd hate myself.

Most of the articles I've read about the real versus fake debate favor the environmental benefit of real trees. Of course,
most of those arguments have been written by tree farmers.
On the other hand, I don't know that I'd trust a petroleum
company's evidence that fake trees are "greener" than real
ones. On the *third* hand, I can't believe that the real versus fake

debate is as important as other environmental issues. Half a million trees a week are cut down to make the nation's Sunday papers; if Americans recycled just 10 percent of their newspapers, we'd save twenty-five million trees annually.

But recycling is not the topic here. For me, the hard thing about a real Christmas tree is that it's dying from the moment you bring it into the house. Christmas-tree experts always say you need to cut off a little disk from the bottom of the trunk before you put it into water, or it seals up permanently and none of the water will ever reach the branches. My husband doesn't believe this—though he sometimes drills holes into the tree base because he likes using his electric drill—and since he's in charge of putting the tree into the stand I don't fight it. (Given the fact that I usually leave the tree outside in its box for several days before we set it up, I don't have much of an argument anyway.) But I always imagine that the poor thing is slowly parching to death. For the first few days, the tree smells fresh and outdoorsy. Then it gradually starts to smell like those fir-balsam-stuffed sachets at gift shops in Maine—aromatic, but not exactly fresh. Then the smell goes away entirely, and ornaments start sliding off the tree's stiff, frail branches. By the time we can steel ourselves to take the tree down, its needles are also showering audibly to the floor. Once, the Boy Scouts, who always pick up old Christmas trees in our town, burst out laughing when they saw the shriveled brown skeleton we'd brought out to their truck.

I'm asking a lot of a fresh tree, I know. My parents always put their tree up on Christmas Eve and take it down on January 6. I like to have ours up through most of December until whenever the Boy Scouts schedule their January pickup. So unless I can make myself switch to fake—or faux, as they say in the trade—I'm doomed to suffer through the tree's slow death.

Whatever I do, the balance in this country has already tilted decisively in favor of fake Christmas trees. About two-thirds of all Christmas-celebrating households in the United States have them already. And as of 2002, about a quarter of those households had stopped setting up any kind of Christmas tree at all. I suppose that since I'm always looking for ways of making the holiday less stressful, that fact should cheer me up. But it doesn't. Maybe I should just shut up and accept the fact although I'll never be satisfied with the tree no matter what I do, it is not a moral issue. Nor, despite my upbringing, is it a matter of family honor. If I'm going to "get my knickers in an uproar" (as a neighbor of ours always puts it), it should be about something that really matters.

Like world peace, or the lights on the tree.

And another thing

The lights! They're so hard to put on!

My Christmas notebook is filled with ideas I've written down to make lighting the tree easier. Some are actually helpful, like PUT LIGHTS ON THE DAY BEFORE TREE-TRIMMING—AVOID RUSHED FEELING, DO BETTER JOB WITH LIGHTS. WILL TAKE AT LEAST 1½ hours. (A year or so later, I changed this to PLAN ON 3 HOURS.) Some seem just to have been pulled out of the air, like 1,000 BULBS IS GOOD NUMBER FOR 7-FOOT TREE. A thousand! What was I thinking? Even Christmas-tree-light websites say you should put on a hundred bulbs for each foot of the tree's height. A thousand would only work if you spread them out from the bottom of the tree in a lacy filigree across the floor.

I see that I also jotted TREE LIGHTS—TOSS OUT ONES WHOSE CORDS HAVE STARTED TO UNRAVEL. BUY 50-LIGHT STRANDS FROM NOW ON—EASIER TO PUT ON. True enough. But then, right after that, I wrote, REMEMBER NEXT YEAR TO DO ONE STRAND AROUND *INSIDE OF TRUNK*.

I didn't actually mean that you should somehow try to get the lights inside the trunk itself. What I meant was that you should tightly wind one strand around and around the trunk, from top to bottom. I didn't have to clarify this in the notebook, because my vision was so clear and bright: I thought that if I could just embrace the trunk in lights, there would be a miraculous shimmer that seemed almost to come from inside the tree itself. It would be like the time Martin Luther saw stars shining through a fir tree in the woods and dreamed up the idea of (sigh) putting candles on it.

I have a feeling that I also just dreamed up this hint, because the following year, when I actually tried it, I realized it would only work if the Christmas tree had no branches. Nevertheless, I persevered, and after perhaps half an hour, the trunk

How Steadfast Are Your Branches!

It was our first Christmas as a married couple—no children yet, but two mature Siamese cats. I seem to recall a very tall bottle of Chianti, or some such period red wine, sitting near the traditionally decorated live tree.

We came home from work to find the cats had attacked the tree and knocked it completely over. On the way down, the tree had obviously hit the tall wine bottle, which also fell over, breaking at the neck. So red wine, horizontal tree, and broken ornaments decorated much of our living room floor. We cleaned it up.

My husband, Allie, stood the tree back up in its red and green metal stand. I watched in awe as he grabbed a hammer and several large nails and proceeded to hammer through the holes in the legs of the stand and right into the hardwood flooring. "There," Allie pronounced as he stood up. "Let's see them knock that over!"

It worked. —J. C.

was tightly wrapped in a string of lights. When this strand was plugged in, it became obvious that you could hardly see the lights at all. When it came time to take the lights off the tree, I realized that unwrapping a Christmas-tree trunk is even more infuriatingly hard than wrapping it. Finally I dragged the tree outside, grabbed one end of the tree-trunk strand, and *whipped* the tree around and around the yard until the strand was off and the tree lay shredded at my feet.

Then I repeated the process the following year, because I was still so sure that if I could get lights wrapped around the trunk *juuuuuuuust riiiiight,* people would gasp with awe. That year, I ended up just chopping the strand off with scissors at the end of the season. But although I have just put the whole struggle on record here, I'd probably try again next Christmas. I know there must be a way of doing this!

Until I figure that out, here are a few *actually* useful tips about lights:

☆ *Plan ahead.* Save yourself from valuable hours of rage next Christmas by taking ten extra minutes *this* Christmas to put your lights away carefully instead of just stuffing them into a box in a big messy tangle. Plug one end of each strand into the other end. Then coil the strand up into a neat circle and secure it with a twist-tie or plastic-bag closer.

☆ *When you uncoil each strand before Christmas, plug it in right away to see if any of the bulbs need replacing.* It's much, much easier to do this on the ground than on the tree. If more than two or three bulbs on the strand don't light up, throw the strand away; it's probably defective. There's nothing more inciteful to murder than having one rogue strand of lights turn off a whole tree's worth.

☆ *Keep the extra bulbs safe.* Don't do what I do and keep all the extra Christmas-tree light bulbs scattered around the bookshelves in your living room. Have a special box for them, and whenever you open a new set of lights, put the spare bulbs into the box. If you can, make it a nice Christmas tin painted with foxes in old-fashioned clothes.

☆ *Do, as I said, put the lights on the tree at least one day before you put on the ornaments.* That will give you a chance to check at night and make sure the lights are evenly placed. (As if you're going to do anything about it if they're not!) But at least if you decide to wiggle them around a little, you won't have a lot of ornaments getting in your way. Allow at least two hours for this job if your tree is six feet tall or more. And take plenty of breaks.

☆ *And if you have tons of money, for heaven's sake, contract the job out.* Do you know how many Christmas-lighting franchises there are? Hundreds! One of the biggest is a company called Christmas Décor, which was created when it occurred to a bright guy in Lubbock, Texas, that people like Ann Hodgman went crazy putting lights on their tree every year and might well pay someone else to do it. The company bills itself as "a Great Add-on Business for: Lawn Care Providers—Nurseries—Irrigation Farms Pest Control Operators—Roofing Companies—Construction Companies—Fence Builders—Pool Services—Florists— Home Services Handyman Trades—Entrepreneurs." All of these are businesses whose winter trade falls off sharply in most parts of the United States, meaning that they have employees who would actually appreciate the chance to wrestle with your Christmas tree. (Not with your crappy lights, though: You have to buy the lights they provide, which cost more but last longer.)

Not only will they come into your house and put the lights on for you, but they will come back after Christmas and take the lights *off*. And store them for you, so that you don't have to do all the complicated coiling-and-twist-tying stuff I described above. And, if you feel like paying for it, they'll bring garland, wreaths, and even the Christmas tree and set them up for you as well. Talk about Santa's elves!

I have a feeling I'd be too embarrassed to hire someone for this job. I hate the thought of some guy cheerfully saying, "There you go, Ms. Hodgman. Have a nice holiday!" while thinking to himself, "Lazy broad won't even put her own lights on the tree." I have an equally strong feeling that if I could just force myself to break the ice (the "hiring-of-a-professional-tree-light-guy" ice, I mean), I'd probably get used to it awfully quickly. Anyway, I'm not going to rule it out if I ever find a pot of gold.

A few words about the ornaments

Every Christmas I struggle between aesthetic considerations and sentiment when we're trimming the tree. I have to wrestle with the fact that if I want the tree to look really beautiful, I can use only a tiny percentage of the ornaments we have. Christmas trees tend to look better when they're not overdecorated, and when each ornament is chosen in relation to the others: All the gold balls, say, are spaced evenly over the tree's surface, and all the ornaments are roughly the same size. And there are no paper chains made by your children when they were in nursery school.

See, that's the real problem: For a tree to look its best, it should only be trimmed by one person—me—and should use none of the ornaments that were handmade by family members. In other words, it should have all the love stripped away.

Well, that's not going to happen in this house. Of course we're going to trim the tree together, which means that the ornaments won't be positioned for maximum effect. Some of the largest, heaviest ones will be bending down the very ends of the branches; some of the nicest ones will be way at the back of the tree where no one can see them. And of course

City Sidewalks. Busy Sidewalks Dressed in Holiday Style...

Last year we decided to buy a big fake tree. After searching our vast Wal-Mart and receiving absolutely no customer service, we finally found the effin' fake trees—for fifty bucks apiece. Defeated, we decided to forego getting a tree from Wal-Mart . . . or *did* we? Outside, they had real trees. So I grabbed a four-foot jobbie, and for a moment, wandered around the sidewalk looking for a person to pay. No one was available to *see* us, let alone take our money. Theresa and I were thinking the same thing. We wordlessly walked with screaming kids and hot tree to our car. —J. K.

we're going to use the ornaments the children made in school, and say (and believe!) that this year's tree is the most beautiful ever. Actually, we start saying that after the first ornament's been put on, because we're wiseacres.

Still, I do usually go over the tree the next morning and move a few of the ornaments around. And every year, when I'm taking the ornaments down, I throw away a few of the really icky ones. *Not* the ones my kids have made, but things like a golf ball with a little stick of fake holly glued to it, and the cartoon-y dog with the googly eyes. Those don't contribute anything, and I don't see why I should have to put up with them.

I'm sure that someday I will have a perfectly beautiful tree. The problem is that it will be a year when I'm alone. Maybe for now I could just buy a tabletop tree in addition to our regular one. The tabletop tree could be my own little project, one I wouldn't have to share. Perhaps I'll realize that decorating a

And a Partridge in a Pear Tree

When our four children were eight and under, we took care of an iguana for two friends in graduate school who were traveling for Christmas. Was the creature named Richard Burton? Our two-and-a-half-year-old daughter, in any case, called it an iganewa. It lived in a glass tank with a screened top, and when not sleeping it spit salt onto the glass. On Christmas morning the iguana looked sick (it later turned out to be shedding its skin). That afternoon, one of us opened the tank to check it, and it got out of its cage and climbed the trunk of our heavily decorated tree. It clung there, spitting. Shrieks and cries. Father to the rescue! With a gingerly gloved clutch, he shoved the homely green beast into a shopping bag. Caged again and spitting, the "iganewa" glared at us. —J. H.

Christmas tree all by yourself isn't so much fun after all. That's the way a woman's magazine story about it would end, anyway. But I bet I'll love it. I'll try it this Christmas and let you know what happens.

Of course, if I had a fake tree it would be pre-lit, and the branches would be so sturdy that even the heaviest ornaments wouldn't bend them. But I'm not letting myself open that thought balloon for another few years, at least.

. . . Or so I thought until recently, when I began to spend more and more covetous hours every day idly clicking through fake tree websites. Finally I decided that as a Christmas writer, I owed it to my readers to order a very expensive fake tree for research purposes. I went to the site of the company whose trees had those "exploded tips of pollinating branches"—the same trees that the *Wall Street Journal* had said were the most realistic you could buy.

Rubbing my hands, I debated the merits of the Noble Fir, the Virginia Pine, and the plain old Classic. Maybe, I thought, I even owed it to my readers to get a twelve-foot tree! We could bend the top four feet over a little bit to make it fit our living room.

Then I chickened out and just ordered a fifteen-dollar swag. And I have to say that it's pretty great. Up close, the needles are a little too shiny and a little too blunt, just like all fake pine needles. And there's also some kind of plastic juniper woven throughout that looks like aquarium foliage. Still, who climbs up over a door to peer closely at a swag? I have all the different kinds of needles in one item, and the pine cones are real. My fake Christmas-tree lust is now satiated, and at a much smaller price than a whole tree would cost. I have nothing left to wish for.

So I've started wishing for a really good pine fragrance to sprinkle on my new pet. I went to an aromatherapy company and bought a tiny bottle of Fir Needle Extract. If I kind of squinch my nostrils tightly, it doesn't smell *too* much like turpentine, and who knows? There may be something much, much better out there if I devote the rest of my days to searching for it.

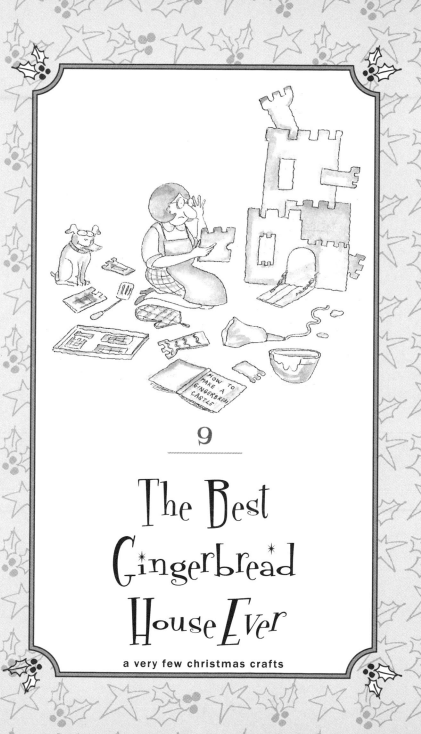

9

The Best Gingerbread House Ever

a very few christmas crafts

Oliver made thick, wobbly clay ashtrays for everyone, though nobody smoked except Father. "They can use 'em for pins and elastic bands and things," Oliver told himself comfortably.

—ELIZABETH ENRIGHT, *THE FOUR-STORY MISTAKE*

Drop in at a craft store some Saturday in December if you want to see a lot of wretched people. Women, mostly, staggering through the wreath section stunned by the mass of choices they have to make. (If only there were three kinds of ribbon instead of three hundred.) A few lost-looking men— what are they doing there? Maybe they have wives who don't know how to drive. Many, many bored children trying to lure their mothers away from the wreath section and over to the sand-craft and paint-spinning kits. Seemingly even more babies and toddlers screaming with rage at how simultaneously boring and tempting every aisle is. And hovering over it all, that sickening smell of scented candles and fake flowers.

I love craft stores, but they're not an easy place to bring children. You can't concentrate on what you need to do (i.e., make the most beautiful wreath or ornament in the history of all craftdom) with a child in tow. People always underestimate the amount of time it will take to pick out their craft supplies. By the time you've chosen all the shapes of tiny wooden ornaments you're going to trim your wreath with (after glazing them with crackle-paint, of course), ninety minutes might easily have passed. It's not fair to expect a child to last that long.

On the other hand, many non-craft-store craft projects can be kind of drab. Often they rely too heavily on construction paper, glitter, and macaroni to produce something you could proudly use as a centerpiece for your Christmas table. Or they veer off into the opposite direction and tell you to cover your Christmas tree with individually applied pearls. ("Use caution, as the glue gun may set the needles aflame.") Strangely, the incredibly complicated projects often end up looking more amateurish than the construction-paper ones.

Here are some Christmas craft suggestions I've seen recently:

☆ Fill a clear globe ornament with popcorn and glitter.

☆ Make a snowman entirely out of white glue. (Didn't the person who dreamed that up realize that white glue dries *clear?*)

☆ Make a wreath out of old CDs. Also, make a wreath out of old jigsaw puzzle pieces. Hey, why don't you make a wreath out of used Kleenexes while you're at it?

Still, I believe it may be illegal to write a Christmas book without including at least a few crafts. So I've narrowed the focus to projects you can do with children. If you want to do beautiful, intricate professional-level crafts on your own— well, my dear, I wouldn't dream of stopping you, and you can find plenty of other books about them. At your local craft store, which you will be visiting *without* your children. And while you're there, you might want to pick up supplies for a couple of the projects in this chapter.

Here are the rules I applied to the following crafts. They all have to be suitable for children from age three to age twelve or so. They have to be fun to make as well as fun to look at. (I remember one nursery-school candlemaking project where the children walked around and around in a grim line, taking turns dipping candle wicks into a vat of wax. A monotonous process, since each candle required thirty dips into the wax before it was bigger than a drinking straw.) They also have to store well and not rot or melt or crumple too easily.

Easy, Easy Gilding

And silvering. *So* easy I wouldn't mention it here at all except that everyone's always impressed with the results—and I've never known anyone besides my family who did this craft routinely. I've read about doing it with real gold leaf paint, but I dunno. I don't see why even my own precious offspring need to be fooling around with real gold.

You'll need:

Cans of gold or silver spray paint (available at hardware stores, Wal-Mart–type stores, and—sorry—craft stores)

A wide variety of nuts in the shell, acorns, pinecones, dried seed pods, bay leaves, and the like

In a well-ventilated area, spread *many* thicknesses of newspaper over a *large* space—preferably the floor, and preferably a basement or garage floor. Put the nuts and other objects to be sprayed in the middle of the newspaper, with a very large newspaper border around them. (Kids sometimes get too exuberant with spray-paint cans, as any large urban area will prove.)

Following the directions on the paint can, spray the nuts

with several smooth, even coatings of paint. Allow to dry for the recommended time; then turn the nuts over and spray them on the unpainted side. Make sure you cover the no-man's land around each nut's "waist" as best you can. If you want to use both gold and silver spray paint, keep the objects to be sprayed in two widely separate areas. (Duh. But I still have to mention it.)

Allow to dry, and you've got one of the prettiest decorations around. You can pile all the nuts and things in a bowl or use them in a centerpiece; they also make a nice present for very young children to give their teachers or grandparents. And you can store them in a coffee can after Christmas; they'll last for years.

As long as we're on the topic of nuts and spray paint, let's also make:

Christmas Mice

Why do walnut shell halves seem so Christmas-y? Is it just because people eat a lot of nuts at Christmas? I don't know, but crafters are inevitably drawn to them. My friend Charmaine gave me one of my favorite Christmas-tree ornaments: a tiny walnut-shell basket filled with tiny balls of yarn and pins stuck into the yarn to represent knitting needles. These mice are awfully sweet, too. One family I know puts them next to Santa's plate of cookies on Christmas Eve so they can have the crumbs when Santa's finished.

If only you could buy half-shells all cleaned out for you! Then I could just say, "Take half a walnut shell . . ." As it is, you'll have slightly better luck if you soak the whole walnuts in salt water overnight. Then you need to stick a sharp, sturdy knife through the middle of each walnut, wiggling it back and forth to pry open the shell. Plan on doing this before you start the kids on the project. Also, plan on wrecking a few.

For each mouse, you will need:

A black Sharpie or other felt-tip marker
1/2 walnut shell, spray-painted gold or silver
2 pistachio nut halves, spray-painted gold or silver
Tiny black beads or peppercorns for the eyes
Narrow gold or silver ribbon for the tail
Craft glue

At the pointy end of the walnut shell, make a black marker dot for the mouse's nose. Glue on the eyes, keeping in mind that they should be much closer to the nose than most kids would put them on. Glue the blunter end of each pistachio shell onto the walnut to make ears—again, keeping in mind that the ears should be only about a quarter-inch in back of the eyes. Glue the tail to the underside of the walnut shell.

If you want the mice to have a race, put a marble under each shell and flick the mice with your finger. They will wobblingly roll across a flat surface, perhaps crashing off the edge of the table onto the floor. Hours of fun! Or seconds, anyway.

Gingerbread Ornaments

This recipe is for what's sometimes called "baker's clay." It produces gingerbread cookies that, though they're not poisonous, are not meant to be eaten. (Now there's a recommendation! "Gingerbread cookies that aren't poisonous!") They look and smell like the real thing, but they're as hard as rocks and will keep forever.

Still, you should hang them out of the dog's reach if you have a dog. Dogs often think inedible stuff is edible. Once one of our dachshunds, though blind and deaf with age, sniffed out and ate a wrapped salt-dough ornament that was hidden under a pile of other presents. Flour, salt, water, and paint were its only ingredients—and even so, Shortie was delighted with it.

He's Making a List and Checking It Twice

My brother and sister-in-law always give me detailed lists of things they want, which I faithfully adhere to. But they never want to listen to *my* list. This year they gave me two useless wooden objects bought at an antique store/warehouse kind of place; they're allegedly "molds" for something. I was delighted to hand back the too-small sweater they'd given my husband, knowing that my mother had given back the huge sweatpants they'd given my dad. My sister-in-law looked at me as if she'd been slapped and said, "I threw out the receipt yesterday." I said, "I'm sure there are lots of people returning gifts without a receipt this week." And I took my wooden objects and we left.
—V. R.

And I can't guarantee that mice will stay away during the off-season, either. Store these in a metal tin.

3 tablespoons solid vegetable shortening

½ cup sugar

½ cup molasses

1 teaspoon baking soda

3½ cups flour

1 teaspoon *each* cloves, ginger, and cinnamon

½ teaspoon salt

¾ cup water, divided

Beat the shortening, sugar, and molasses until fluffy. In a large bowl, stir together the dry ingredients. Beat in the shortening mixture in three parts; after each third is added, beat in

¼ cup of the water. This makes a very stiff dough, and you may need to end up mixing it with your hands.

Chill the dough overnight, wrapped in plastic.

Preheat the oven to 350°. Cut the dough into 4 pieces, and knead each piece slightly to warm it. On waxed paper or baking parchment, roll out each piece of dough ¼ thick. Cut into desired shapes with cookie cutters. Use a drinking straw or skewer to punch a hole into the center of each cookie if you plan to hang it from the tree.

Bake the cookies on greased sheets for 20 minutes. When they're done, turn the oven off but leave the cookies inside until they're completely cool. Then put them on racks and stash them somewhere for three days, until they're completely hardened.

The cookies may be sealed with acrylic glaze if you wish, and may also be painted with acrylic paints. If you use the paints with kids, I'd stick to red and white as being more frosting-y looking. I'd also advise the kids to use the paint sparingly, but good luck on that.

Decorated Votive Candle-Holders (and Votive Candles)

You can't have too many candles at Christmas—except for the scented kind. Even one of those is too many.

I live in such a small town—fewer than four thousand of us—that if I can find something at my grocery store, you can probably find it at yours. And if you have access to a big huge supermarket like most people I know, you can *certainly* find it. The "it" in this case is glass votive candle holders. There are seventeen kinds at my grocery store! They're cheap and sturdy, and pretty in themselves—a perfect thing for kids to work on.

What you do is this: You or your children pick out a few of the ones you like best. Then you decorate the rims with any of the following:

☆ *Tiny metallic stickers.* If you live in my town, just go across the street from the grocery store and get your stickers at the Hickory Stick Bookshop, which has a great selection. But fortunately metallic stickers are not hard to find. Regular stickers would work okay, but metallic ones are much better for this purpose.

☆ *Small, bright-colored buttons and beads.* Use craft glue—the tackier, the better. There's even a brand called "Tacky."

☆ *Fake pearls.* (An amazingly effective decoration, by the way. Recently, Oscar de la Renta introduced evening bags covered with big faux pearls. Why didn't I think of that?) Again, use the thickest, "tackiest" craft glue you can find.

☆ *Dots of glitter glue.* And I mean regularly spaced DOTS, not big, blobby, wavering lines. But then I find it very, very hard to relinquish control over this kind of project. I want to make all the candle holders myself! I suppose your children's grandparents will still love the candleholders even if they've been dipped in glitter glue. Just give them ample time to dry before wrapping them.

Now, you can either choose color-coordinated votive candles for these, or you can decorate your own. You can also decorate your own votives as a separate project, without bothering with candleholders.

I hesitate to suggest a project that requires you to order something from a specific catalog, but the Candle Decorating Waxes in the HearthSong catalog (www.hearthsong.com; telephone 800-325-2502) are hard to find elsewhere and greatly superior to most decorating wax. For many years I was a one-room Sunday School teacher, and decorating Christmas candles with HearthSong wax sheets was one of the kids' favorite things to do. In fact, the first year we tried it, the kids got so absorbed that they were all silently working as their parents came to retrieve them at the end of the class. *That* didn't happen often, I can tell you.

I use boxes of "household votives" for kids to decorate, because they're so cheap that each child can make quite a few. But any candle will work. You pinch off bits of the beeswax sheets, warm them in your hands for a few seconds, and then simply press them onto the candle and hold them down for a few seconds more to "glue" them on. Some of the boys I've seen work on this project have preferred to wrap the candles in whole sheets of beeswax, which has always been fine with me as long as they don't use up all the red, gold, and purple sheets. In Sunday School I had to ration those colors.

If you like doing crafts with your kids, you should probably be on the HearthSong mailing list. They have all kinds of wonderful seasonal projects, along with toys with more imagination and integrity than what you'll find at big chain stores. Now that my own children are seventeen and twenty, I often find myself making excuses to draft *other* people's children into doing HearthSong crafts with me.

The Gingerbread House

Why isn't this one in the recipe chapter? Because in my family, we've refined gingerbread-house making to the point where the house is no longer edible. Who cares about the *house* part of a gingerbread house,

What Can I Give Him, Poor as I Am?

One year I gave my sister-in-law a very cool and quite expensive art book. She asked if it had come from a nearby design store. When I said yes, she said, "Well, then, you paid too much for it." You're welcome!—R. M. M.

after all? Everyone just likes the candy that decorates it. When Laura was about one and a half, David once caught her in the dining room picking bits of candy off the gingerbread house. "Dave, go out," she ordered him.

Using a big cardboard box for the house allows you much more decorating freedom. The most problematic part of the structure—getting the sides to stand up without collapsing— has already been done for you. You don't have to be afraid that you'll press that one last gumdrop into place and have the whole thing topple inward. You can also cut more intricate shapes in cardboard more easily than in gingerbread. If you want actual "gingerbread trim" to make the house look Victorian, for example, you can cut separate cardboard strips into the pattern you like. And if your children are quite young and you want to keep things simple—well, cutting four square windows in a box is manageable for even the least crafty types.

David and my sister Cathy once made a gingerbread house in which every side was completely different. When they were all done, Cathy gazed with shining eyes at the side she had just finished. Then she rotated the house so she could study another side. "Changing the channel?" David asked.

There's no reason to involve your children when you make the actual house. I say this not only because there's a huge part of me that hates relinquishing control of my projects but also because this is the boring part for kids. (It's also more dangerous, since it requires a sharp knife for the windows and roof.) Present your kids with the finished structure to decorate and everyone will be much happier.

I can't really give you quantities, because I don't know a) how big you want the house to be and b) how much candy you're going to let the kids eat as they work. But here are the bare bones of what you'll need:

Two corrugated cardboard boxes

A sharp knife or a strong pair of scissors

Two cans of milk-chocolate frosting (the most gingerbread-y looking, but

of course you can use any kind you want); one can of white icing if
you're going to set the house on a base or a big cookie sheet

Assorted candy for decorating the house. A few suggestions:

Hard candy for the windows: assorted Lifesavers, sourballs, or Jolly
Ranchers for stained-glass windows, or those bluish "ice mints" for
regular glass

Andes Mints for roof tiles and pavement

Thin pretzel sticks or Frosted Mini-Wheats if you'd rather have a
"thatched" roof

Red licorice sticks to cover corners

Hershey's Kisses for roof turrets

M & Ms or red-hots for doorknobs and other trim

Marshmallows if you want snowmen standing outside the house

Toothpicks for sticking the marshmallow snowmen together

And so on and so on. Just go to the candy section in your
store and pick stuff out, for goodness' sake. And if you want
inspiration, get a couple of Christmas magazines. *Good House-
keeping*'s Christmas issue always has lots of gingerbread house
photos.

So: Start with the corrugated cardboard box. You'll need a
second box to make the roof. If you are me, you'll also make a
steeple for this roof out of the second box and convert the
house into a gingerbread church, instead. When I'm in charge
of the gingerbread house, I always make a church instead of a
house. (I like to make stained-glass windows out of hard
candy, and why would there be stained-glass windows on a
house?)

Using a sharp knife or very durable scissors, cut the kinds
of windows and doors you want in the box. Make the kind of
roof you want with the second box, but don't put it on until
the windows are done. A big sheet of cardboard makes a good
base for the house.

These Wonderful Things Are the Things We Remember All Through Our Lives!

Our first married Christmas (fifty-one years ago) was very strange and emotional for me. I was determined to start traditions for my husband and me similar to those that had existed in my family. Since I had no relatives in town, there were quite a few "adopted" aunts and uncles for whom my mother had always made Christmas candy. I drew up a list of friends and put together some cute gold-paper cornucopias of my special chocolate cookies for them. Then I dragged my new husband on a Christmas Eve delivery venture. At house after house we found no one at home, and we sadly left the cookies hanging on the doorknobs. At the last stop someone finally opened the door. We were asked in to find all the friends we had called upon, having a festive Christmas Eve together without us!—C. O.

Candy windows are something the children will like helping with, perhaps the day before you make the house. Preheat the oven to 300° and cover two cookie sheets with baking parchment or greased foil. Different hard candies melt at varying rates (and melt to varying thicknesses), so experiment with a piece or two before you plan your windows. I like to put contrasting colors next to each other so that they melt into varicolored panels. For plain glass, six to eight ice mints placed in a rectangle will work well. Remember that you'll need the windows to be at least an inch wider than the window openings you've cut in the cardboard, so that you can "glue" them on with frosting. And plan on making many more windows than you'll need, partly because it's fun to make them and partly because a few of them will break when you're installing them.

After experimenting with a couple of samples, lay out the rest of the hard candies on the lined cookie sheets. Bake them for 8 to 10 minutes, checking frequently to make sure they have not begun to bubble or burn. A few tiny bubbles are inevitable, though. You'll have to pretend the panes are made of very thick old-fashioned glass.

Cool the candy panes completely; then peel them off the cookie sheets. Now comes an unpleasantly finicky step for which you may not want small witnesses. Reaching inside the house, spread a layer of icing around the outline of each window opening. "Glue" the windowpanes inside the house by pressing them to the icing border you've made. Once they're stuck on, *never touch them again*. You won't be able to re-install them once the roof is attached to the house.

Attaching the roof is most easily done with masking tape. Don't worry; you'll be covering it with frosting, so it will never show.

Depending on your children's ages, they can help frost the house or not. If they're too little to help, maybe they can frost the cardboard base with white icing. ("You're doing the most important part," you can tell them. "The snow!") Or they can unwrap the candy you're going to decorate the house with. In any case, set the house on the iced base (if you're using a base), then frost the house and roof thickly with the canned frosting. Ignore the horrible cheesy smell of the frosting; it will dissipate in a couple of hours.

Now take the decorating candy and go nuts. If your children are bickerers, it's often less stressful to assign each child to one side of the house. You can just hover over all and make helpful suggestions on the order of "Are you sure that's where you want to put that?" until your children make *you* go out of the room.

Makes one house, serving one family's picking-off-candy needs for several days.

Russian Snowfall

My brother Ned's wife, Tamara, is Russian, and has introduced us to many wonderful Russian Christmas traditions. Inspired by Tamara, my brother once dressed up as Father Frost (the Russian equivalent of Santa) and stole into my children's rooms early Christmas morning to pay them a visit when they were quite young. He glided in and out in grave silence. The kids were more confused than anything else, because Ned and Tamara had excitedly put his "costume" together at the very last minute. I think Ned had a beard made out of white curling ribbon and was wearing a bathrobe. But still, it was impressive.

This "snow" is *much* more impressive. In fact, it's amazingly beautiful. It looks like a snowfall coming down from the ceiling and is very easy to do, though time-consuming. You should plan it for a *small* room unless you are extremely enthusiastic; Ned and Tamara do one in the vestibule of their house, and I put ours in the little alcove by our back door. You should also realize that your children may grow tired of working on the project unless you're all doing something else while working, like watching a Christmas movie. But I can't resist including it because it's so striking, and you'll never see anything else like it unless you visit Ned and Tamara in Moscow.

Just pace yourself. You and the kids are not going to get the whole thing done between supper and bathtime.

You will need:

A reel or two of white string
Two spools of white thread
A bag of cotton balls (real cotton, not the polyester kind)
Tacks or pushpins

After you've decided which small room you're going to tackle, tack or pin lengths of string across the ceiling in straight lines that are one foot apart. (This is a job for you, obviously, not for your children.) These are the "anchor" strings.

Now figure out how long a piece of thread should be to hang from an "anchor" string just above the height of your head. Cut about a hundred pieces of thread to this length. Then, says my brother, "you squeench off pieces of cotton from cotton balls"—those are the snowflakes—"and from these you squeench off a tiny piece that serves to hold the

He Was Dressed All in Fur, from His Head to His Foot...

On Christmas, we would open our stockings in the den, a rarely used room at my parents' house. It had a big fireplace and we always had a fire that morning. After breakfast, my mother went into the den to light the fire, but the room soon backed up with smoke.

It turned out the cause was a raccoon nest at the top of the chimney. So my father, who hunts, grabbed his shotgun and shot the dazed-looking raccoon, who was crawling out of the top of the chimney. The wounded raccoon fell out of the chimney and hit a series of pine branches on the way down until *whump*, there it was in its death throes on the patio, right outside the kitchen window.

My father then decided that the raccoon tail would make a delightful gift for a young boy he knew. So he took a hatchet, chopped off the raccoon's tail, and left it in our back entryway. Later that day, our miniature dachshund, who had been strangely absent most of the day, turned up groaning and gasping and absolutely HUGE. And yes, sure enough, the chopped-off raccoon tail was missing!—P. R.

snowflake to the thread." (Ned actually said "snowclump," which is just what a man would call a snowflake.)

I was naturally curious about the squeenching process. Ned explained that it's basically just that you pinch off a wisp of cotton about a quarter of an inch long, and wrap it gently around the thread. You don't have to tie it on; it will stick to the thread by itself. Ned says, "Just rub it between your fingers until it clumps around the thread and is well attached." The wisps of cotton will look more natural if you keep them wispy rather than rolling them into balls—but balls are okay, too. There are all kinds of snowflakes in the world, after all.

Put the flakes on each thread at four- or five-inch intervals—and put one flake on or near the bottom of each thread. As you finish a thread, lay it straight out on a table and don't let the cat get it.

Then tie the threads to the "anchor strings" at regular intervals. Make more threads if you need them, of course. I was only saying one-hundred because my brother had weirdly said to use "about ninety or so." Once again, he has *wrecked* Christmas.

10

Beyond Fruitcake

a very few christmas recipes

Cream together: 2 T. butter, 2½ cups sugar, ½ teaspoon anise oil. Add 6 eggs. Drop bowl in middle. Cry.

—FAMILY PFEFFERNUSSE RECIPE EDITED BY MY SISTER NELIE

There are already tons of Christmas cookbooks on the market. We don't need more of them. If anything, we need *fewer*.
But I could never write a Christmas book without including a
few of the recipes that mean the most to me and my family at
Christmastime. Not things like roast beef or crown roast of
pork or other big, protein centerpieces like that. You probably
already have recipes for those—and if you don't, you can easily find them. The recipes here are for some of the "extras." A
couple of side dishes; a couple of cookie recipes; a dessert or
two. That kind of thing. I'm giving you just ten—one for almost each day of Christmas.

Which reminds me: You probably have lots of favorite holiday recipes already, but you shouldn't save them specifically for
December 25. Nowadays, when most of us have way too much
to eat way too much of the time, a gajillion-course meal with

tons of side dishes is not as meaningful as it once was. In the spirit of spreading Christmas a little thinner, think about serving some of your family's favorites throughout December and January—and not all at one huge meal, but simply as a "featured attraction" at a regular meal. That way, you can keep the Christmas feeling going for longer and not feel like a glutton doing it.

Stained Glass Terrine
Serves 8.

I wanted to give you a great Christmas breakfast dish, and for days I tried to find the best strata recipe out there. You know strata: the perfect Christmas breakfast, because it needs to be made the night before and you can just pop it into the oven on Christmas morning? The one where you make layers of bread cubes, cheese, and sausage, and then pour a custard over them and let them chill overnight before baking?

There are dozens of recipes for strata—you probably already have a couple—but I wasn't able to find one that fabulously improved upon the basics. I mean, how can you really go wrong with *any* strata recipe? They're all good. You can improve most of them by adding more cheese and sausage than the recipe calls for; using crusty French or Italian or sourdough bread instead of regular supermarket bread; and adding dried mustard and other flavorings to the egg custard you pour over the layers before refrigerating them for the night.

There. That's *that* recipe taken care of. But we still need a breakfast recipe. How about this great fruit terrine, which must be made ahead of time, and is light, fresh tasting, and beautiful on the plate? A perfect addition, and corrective, to the delicious but rich Christmas breakfast most of us eat—and more interesting than plain old cut-up fruit.

4 large pink or ruby-red grapefruits (or two 1-pound, 8-ounce jars of cut-up grapefruits, with juice—available in the produce section of most supermarkets)

4 navel oranges

Additional pink grapefruit juice, if needed

⅓ cup sugar

½ cup orange juice

2 envelopes unflavored gelatin

½ cup frozen unsweetened raspberries

At least one day before you'll be serving the recipe, spray the inside of a 9 × 5" loaf pan with cooking spray. Line the pan with plastic wrap, leaving a 6-inch overhang on each side.

With a sharp knife, carefully peel the grapefruits and the oranges. Make sure to get all the white pith, scraps of rind, and outer membranes from the fruit. Then, over a strainer or colander set above another bowl, cut the fruits into segments with the same sharp knife, leaving the segments whole and letting them fall into the strainer. This is finicky work, I know, but think how much more annoying it would be if you were doing it with limes! Discard the seeds and inner membranes that separate the segments. You will be dismayed at how much fruit you weren't able to cut off, but don't worry. If this is the most wasteful you get this Christmas, you're lucky.

Set the fruit, in its strainer, on a plate. Measure the grapefruit and orange juice that has collected in the bottom of the bowl. Add enough of the extra pink-grapefruit juice to measure 2⅓ cups of juice. Pour the juice into a small saucepan and stir in the sugar.

Pour the orange juice into a small bowl, and stir in the gelatin. Leave it to soften while you go onto the next step. (The reason you need to use orange juice for this step, even though you have all that grapefruit juice sitting around, is that the acid in straight grapefruit juice might inhibit the gelatin's strength. It also might not, but if it did, think how mad you'd be!)

Bring the grapefruit juice and sugar to a boil. Lower the heat and simmer for about 15 minutes, until the liquid has been reduced by ⅓. Remove the saucepan from the heat and

Gone Away Is the Bluebird. Here to Stay Is a New Bird...

Many, many, many years ago, when my first child was *in utero*, Christmas was looming, and I was feeling awful. We had asked some college friends to Christmas dinner. The day before, I stuffed the damn turkey. (In those days we all stuffed turkeys days ahead, and no one got botulism—we were probably immune from all the casually canned string beans we had ingested as children.)

I woke early the next morning feeling pretty rotten and asked my husband, Chuck, to go downstairs and put the turkey in the oven. I had covered it with a piece of an old dress to keep it moist while it cooked. I can see the dress now, a lovely lavender cotton with little flecks of green and a full skirt. From time to time I asked Chuck to look at the turkey. He said it was fine—and the juice was getting a rich color. I pulled myself together about an hour before everyone was to arrive and was horrified to see that not only was the juice a rich color but the turkey was truly purple. Nothing to do but pour lots of drinks and then serve it proudly, announcing I had used a new recipe involving plums. No one cared by then, and it tasted just fine.—A. B.

whisk in the softened gelatin mixture until thoroughly dissolved.

Carefully add the citrus sections and reserved whole frozen raspberries to the loaf pan, and carefully pour the citrus juice-gelatin mixture over them. Bring the overhanging plastic wrap up to cover, and set the loaf pan into the refrigerator to chill overnight.

The next morning, unmold the terrine onto a cutting board. Peel away the plastic wrap. Cut the terrine into slices with a very sharp knife, lay them decoratively on a platter, and serve.

By the way, if you don't want to bother with the unmolding and slicing routine, you can just chill the terrine in a bowl or individual ramekins—only then you won't be able to call it a terrine.

Bishop's Bread

I believe it's traditional, in Christmas cookbooks, to include one fruitcake recipe with the disclaimer, "No, but this fruitcake really is good!" Then what follows is a regular fruitcake with, perhaps, some jam added to make it even darker and stickier than usual.

Bishop's Bread, the engine that has driven the Hodgman Christmases for as long as I can remember, *really is* good—mainly because it's not really a fruitcake. It's more like a pound-cake crossed with a teacake—a buttery loaf cake with, yes, a little fruit and some nuts in it, but nothing that drags it down. And the miniature chocolate chips make all the difference.

My mother makes billions of Bishop's Breads every Christmas—well, millions, anyway. Before you could buy miniature chocolate chips in regular stores, she used to have to get them at a baking-supply store downtown. She would come home with *huuuuuuge* plastic bags of tiny chocolate chips and store them in an extra refrigerator in the cellar, where they were very tempting to us children. This fridge had an old-fashioned door that clicked shut, rather than a modern magnetic door. Once my little brother came upstairs crying, "I hurt my hand in the chocolate—I mean the refrigerator!" He then hurried to explain that he had not gone near the chocolate chips but had just somehow pinched his fingers in the door, which might have been more convincing if his face hadn't been covered with chocolate. Anyway, when we were coming up with memories of my mom for her birthday, those tiny chocolate chips from Atlantic Supply were the first thing all four of us remembered.

Over the years Mum and I have begun to think that although there's not a lot of candied fruit in this recipe, there's still too much. We're toying with the idea of replacing the candied fruit with chopped dried apricots and dried cherries. I think this change will lodge the recipe permanently in twenty-first-century Christmases.

12 tablespoons (1½ sticks) unsalted butter

¾ cup sugar

4 eggs

1 teaspoon vanilla extract

2 cups all-purpose flour, divided

½ cup *each* currants; chopped walnuts or pecans; and miniature chocolate chips

½ cup finely chopped candied fruit—or ¼ cup each finely chopped dried apricots and finely chopped dried sour cherries

2 teaspoons baking powder

¼ teaspoon salt

Place a rack in the middle of oven and preheat to 350°. Grease two 8 × 4" loaf pans and line them with waxed paper, greased foil, or baking parchment cut to fit. (A greased 6" springform pan makes a darling presentation as well if you want one of the cakes to be round.)

In a large bowl, cream the butter and sugar. Add the eggs and vanilla and mix until light and fluffy. In a separate bowl, toss the currants, nuts, chocolate chips, and candied fruit with one cup of the flour until evenly coated. In another little bowl, stir together the remaining 1 cup of flour, the baking powder, and the salt. Add the fruit mixture to the egg mixture and beat well; then thoroughly stir in the flour mixture.

Spoon the batter into the 2 prepared pans, smoothing the tops. Bake the loaves for 45 minutes, switching their places halfway through the baking time. Cool for 15 minutes in the pans; then turn the loaves out onto racks and finish cooling before wrapping in plastic wrap and then in foil. Store in the refrigerator for up to a month, preferably in one of the fruit and vegetable drawers.

Mulled Cranberry Potion? Brew? Juice?
Makes 2 quarts, serving 4 to 6.

Let's go with "juice." I know that homemade hot chocolate is traditional with Christmas breakfast, but good hot chocolate is practically a meal in itself. And it's certainly overkill as part of the standard 10,000-calorie Christmas breakfast. Why not have hot chocolate on one of the other twelve days of Christmas, and switch to this mulled cranberry juice for December 25? Kids like it; it can be made ahead and reheated, unlike hot chocolate; and even if you decide to float a blob of whipped cream on top, it's nowhere near as thick and murderous as hot chocolate.

This recipe does not contain alcohol, because frankly on Christmas morning I don't think that's a good idea. If you want to add rum, brandy, Calvados, or applejack, you know what to do without my help.

It seems crazy to buy cranberry juice cocktail for this when you can make your own pure cranberry juice so easily and cheaply, and can sweeten it to your own taste. (My little tiny grocery store sells 100 percent unsweetened cranberry juice in the "bottled juice" section, and that's what I use.) If you can't bear the thought of that extra step, cranberry juice cocktail will work nicely too—but don't add any sugar. You might even want to add a little lemon juice to perk things up.

8 cups unsweetened cranberry juice (see note, p. 151)

⅔ cup granulated sugar, or to taste

2 cinnamon sticks, broken in half, plus 8 more whole sticks for the mugs

6 whole cardamom pods or ½ teaspoon ground cardamom

1 whole nutmeg

½ teaspoon ginger (or a 2-inch chunk of fresh gingerroot)

1 whole unpeeled orange, stuck with 12 whole cloves

Sweetened whipped cream for garnish (optional)

Now Bring Us Some Figgy Pudding

My first Christmas after I got married was my first Christmas away from cold and snow. My wife's parents lived in Los Angeles, and we went to their house on Christmas Eve for dinner with a huge number of family and friends. I was comforted because the catered dinner included only food that one associates with cold weather—beef Wellington, roast turkey with stuffing—instead of fruit salad or sushi. Dessert was plum pudding, and my mother-in-law passed around a big silver gravy boat telling all her guests that they absolutely had to put "lots of vanilla sauce" on top of their pudding. Everyone poured on the sauce and eagerly dug into the dessert. It was not the taste I was expecting. The dining room fell silent. Finally one brave guest swallowed and said, "Are you sure this is vanilla sauce?" The hostess picked up the gravy boat, dipped her finger in, tasted it and said, "Oh my God, this is the extra Caesar salad dressing!"—B. S.

In a large pot, mix all the ingredients except the orange and whipped cream. Taste the mixture to see if it's sweet enough; then have one of the kids drop in the orange, making a big splash all over the stovetop. Stirring frequently, bring the juice to a boil; then lower the heat and simmer, uncovered, for 30 minutes.

With a slotted spoon, carefully remove the orange, the cinnamon sticks, the cardamom pods and, if you used it, the fresh ginger from the pot. Ladle the juice into mugs and give each mug a cinnamon stick to stir with if you feel like it, and some sweetened whipped cream if ditto.

<u>Note:</u> To make your own unsweetened cranberry juice, bring 10 cups water to a boil with 3 12-ounce bags of fresh or frozen cranberries. Lower the heat to a simmer and cook the mixture for 15 minutes. Strain through a fine sieve without pushing down on the fruit pulp; you want the juice to be clear, not cloudy. Measure out 8 cups.

The "Cider Treatment" for Poultry or Pork
Serves 4 to 6.

Don't you always associate cider and apples with the holidays? I do. My Christmas fix is not completely satisfied unless I use this twofold "treatment" a couple of times in December and January. What you start with is a marinade that is actually a "flavor brine"—but I'm calling it a marinade so as not to scare you off. You mix cider, salt, and spices and use it to marinate (or brine) poultry or pork for at least 24 hours. During that time, the salt helps the protein strands in the meat absorb liquid so that it will be much juicier. (Believe it or not, there are three possible chemical explanations for this process.)

Then you dust the meat with a spicy flour that gives it a deliciously unusual coating, and bake it as usual—except that you add more cider and some apples during the last third of the baking time. And there you go!

I would say, myself, that this recipe isn't quite fancy enough to use on plain chicken pieces for Christmas dinner. For Christmas, I'd use it with Cornish hens or a capon, or a turkey if I were the kind of person who ever served turkey at Christmas. WHICH I'M NOT, as I've told you on practically every page of this book.

The basic brining formula is 1 gallon of liquid to 1 cup of kosher salt or ½ cup of regular salt. If you're brining a turkey or a large cut of pork (a crown roast, say), you can increase the recipe to whatever will cover the meat. But then you have the problem of where you're going to chill this massive container of liquid. Do you have a spare refrigerator, as I do, or a nice cold porch, as I do (at Christmas, anyway)? If not, you can always put the meat into a plastic garbage bag; add enough liquid to submerge the meat completely; seal the bag tightly; put it into another plastic garbage bag and seal that; and then clear all the vegetables out of the crisper drawer and put the meat in there instead. (The vegetables will be fine at room temperature for a day.) Anyway, be aware that this challenge lies ahead if you're brining a large cut of meat.

For the marinade:

> ½ gallon cider, preferably unpasteurized
> ½ cup kosher salt or ¼ cup regular salt
> 2 whole cinnamon sticks, broken into pieces

For the chicken:

> 6 half-breasts of chicken (about 3 pounds)
> 2 cups flour
> 2 tablespoons ginger
> 1 tablespoon cinnamon
> Salt and pepper, to taste
> 1 cup cider (not from the marinade)
> 2 tablespoons light brown sugar, packed
> 2 Golden Delicious apples, peeled, cored, and sliced

The day before you plan to serve the chicken, stir the marinade ingredients together until the salt is completely dissolved. Plop in the chicken breasts, cover the bowl or pot or whatever you're using, and refrigerate for 24 hours.

Preheat the oven to 350°. Drain the chicken pieces and pat them dry. In a pie pan or similar flat dish, stir together the flour, ginger, and cinnamon. Flip each piece of chicken around in the seasoned flour, pressing flour into the surface of the meat on both sides and knocking off the excess. Put the chicken skin-side up in a 9 × 13" baking dish. Sprinkle with salt and pepper and bake for 45 minutes.

In a small bowl, stir together 1 cup cider and the brown sugar. Add the sliced apples to the pan of chicken and pour the sweetened cider over all. Bake for 25 more minutes, spooning the cider sauce over the chicken at least three times. Serve the chicken immediately with noodles or rice.

Roasted Lemon-Garlic Green Beans
Serves 4 to 6.

Don't vegetables sometimes seem like the last straw at Christmas dinner? Even though they make all the difference between a regular meal and a great one? The best thing about these beans, besides how good they taste, is that they can be made the day before and can be served at room temperature. They could be served cold, too, I suppose, but room temperature is better. I always serve them that way; in fact, I always serve them, period. Ever since I tried this recipe, I've made my green beans this way—and we're not sick of them yet.

The only hard thing about this recipe is the quantity you need to make. In roasting, the beans shrink to half their size, so you need to start out with a lot of them to make a respectable showing at the table. Get the kids or your houseguests to help trim them.

2 pounds green beans, trimmed

½ cup corn or olive oil

4 large garlic cloves, put through a press

6 sprigs fresh thyme, cut in half

Salt, to taste

Juice of 1 large lemon

Put a rack in the top third of the oven and preheat the oven to 475°. Line a large rimmed cookie sheet with foil.

In a large bowl, toss the beans with all the other ingredients. Spread them out all over the cookie sheet so that they're in a single layer (or as close to one as possible). Roast them for 15 to 20 minutes, stirring them carefully every 5 minutes. They should be shriveled and lightly browned in many places. Pick out the thyme sprigs. Serve hot, room temperature, or cold.

Upgraded Cranberry Compote
Makes 3 cups, serving 6 to 8.

I know you have a recipe for regular cranberry sauce—either that, or you use the canned stuff. (I'm not criticizing you for that. Canned is fine.) But this is dressier and more unusual, and it's better than regular cranberry sauce if you're having something besides turkey. It's perfect with pork, ham, roast beef, and venison; it gives you that cranberry note without duplicating a Thanksgiving food. As everyone who knows me knows, I think it's silly to repeat Thanksgiving foods at Christmas, only six weeks later.

½ pound fresh pearl onions, unpeeled

1 tablespoon unsalted butter

¾ cup sugar

½ cup white-wine vinegar or champagne vinegar, divided

1 cup dry white wine

1 teaspoon lemon juice, or more to taste

½ teaspoon salt

⅛ teaspoon each nutmeg and cinnamon

1 tablespoon fresh-grated orange rind

1 cup dried unsweetened sour cherries

½ cup water

½ pound (2 cups) fresh or frozen cranberries (don't thaw them if they're frozen)

Bring a medium saucepan of water to boil. Add the onions and cook for 1 minute. Drain and peel them. Dry out the saucepan with a piece of paper towel and melt the butter in it. Cook the onions, stirring gently, for 1 minute. Add the sugar and 1 tablespoon of the vinegar to the mixture and cook, stirring, until the syrup turns a light caramel color. This will take about 15 minutes. Don't worry if the onions fall apart a little bit.

Stir in the rest of the vinegar, the wine, the lemon juice, and the salt. Keep your face averted from the saucepan, since the mixture will steam and bubble quite a lot. Add the spices, the orange rind, and the dried cherries. Cook the mixture over low heat, stirring frequently, for 45 minutes. The liquid should be thick and syrupy.

Add the cranberries and the water and bring the mixture to a slow boil. Cook it until the cranberries have all popped—about 10 to 15 minutes. Cool completely and serve at room temperature. (The compote will keep in the refrigerator for a week.)

Eggnog Cream
Serves 8.

Elegant, smooth, rich, and rum-filled, this is one dessert your children probably won't like. But there's not much point to making it if you leave out the rum. You'll like it, anyway. The kids can have a candy cane or something.

1 tablespoon (1 envelope) unflavored gelatin

½ cup cold water

6 large egg yolks

1 cup sugar

½ cup dark rum

2 cups (16 ounces) heavy cream

Pinch of salt

2 ounces high-quality bittersweet chocolate, grated or shaved with a
vegetable peeler

In a small saucepan stir the gelatin into the water. Let the mixture soak while you beat the egg yolks in a medium bowl until light and fluffy. Add the sugar to the yolks gradually, beating all the time, and then beat for 3 to 5 minutes, until the mixture becomes very pale and smooth.

Put the saucepan with the gelatin over the lowest possible heat and stir just until the mixture is dissolved. Do not allow the mixture to become really hot, and certainly don't let it simmer. Pour the dissolved gelatin mixture over the egg yolks in a thin, slow stream, beating constantly. Cool the mixture and stir in the rum.

In a chilled bowl, with clean, chilled beaters, whip the cream with the salt until it holds stiff peaks. Fold the whipped cream into the cooled egg mixture. Spoon

Here We Come A-Wassailing

While we were all gathered around my aunt's piano enjoying a romp through the Christmas portion of "Messiah" (which my family could manage in all four parts, thank you), a candle spilled in the kitchen, setting fire to the tablecloth and tabletop. We were blissfully ignorant until someone mentioned a bright light in the kitchen. Well, weren't we surprised! We used eggnog as the extinguisher. Thank God there wasn't more hooch in it.—M. S.

half the dessert into a bowl; top it with half the grated chocolate. Repeat with the second half of the dessert and the rest of the grated chocolate. Chill the eggnog cream for at least 4 hours, or up to 24 hours.

Cranberry Ice Cream
Makes 1 quart.

You do need an ice-cream maker for this, but it's so good that you really might as well go out and buy one for yourself. Christmas is coming, after all. Oh, and you need a food mill as well. (Not a baby-food mill; a regular one.) Sorry! But really, this ice cream is worth it. As of this writing, ice cream makers and food mills are available by the hundreds on eBay—the latter often for less than ten dollars.

Packed into a sealed container, this will keep for five days. So why not make it way ahead?

4 cups fresh or frozen cranberries, picked over

½ cup fresh lemon juice

1 ¼ cups sugar

6 large egg yolks

½ cup (8 tablespoons) unsalted butter

1½ cups heavy cream

½ cup milk

Pinch of salt

Put the cranberries, lemon juice, and sugar into a medium saucepan over medium heat. Bring to a simmer and cook for 20 minutes, stirring frequently. All the cranberries should have popped, and the mixture should be very soft and thick. Transfer the mixture to a food mill and puree; discard the skins and seeds.

In a clean saucepan, whisk the cranberry puree and the egg yolks until smooth. Over low heat, stirring constantly with a wooden or plastic spoon, cook the mixture for 10 to 15 minutes, or until it is very thick.

Remove the saucepan from the heat and whisk in the butter a tablespoon at a time. Cool to room temperature; then stir in the heavy cream, milk, and salt. Chill the mixture for several hours or overnight. Freeze in an ice cream maker according to the manufacturer's directions. Transfer to a sealed container and allow to ripen in the freezer for several hours (or up to five days) before serving.

Peppernuts ("Sucking Cookies")
Makes dozens and dozens of tiny cookies.
Please don't ask me to count them!

This recipe is from my mother's friend Sue Olson, who got it from relatives in Nebraska. My brother and sisters and I loved these cookies when we were kids. They're smooth, glossy, and hard—so hard you have to suck them for a while before you dare to bite them. (Especially when you are an adult with crowns and bridgework.) This adds a fascinating new wrinkle to the whole "eating cookies" business. But when I first saw the recipe I was afraid my kids wouldn't like them. Anise extract? Allspice? So I made a few changes, and I was right. My kids didn't like the cookies—with my changes, I mean. When I went back to Sue's real recipe, they loved them as much as I had.

Wash your hands before you make this. You'll need them. And take off any rings unless you like getting dough in the prongs.

    2 cups sugar
    2 cups dark corn syrup
    ½ cup milk
    ½ cup shortening
    1 teaspoon cinnamon
    ½ teaspoon each allspice and cloves

1 teaspoon lemon extract
½ teaspoon anise extract
2 teaspoons baking powder
5½ to 6½ cups flour

In a large saucepan, bring the sugar, corn syrup, and milk to a boil. Stir in the shortening until it has melted. Cool the mixture for half an hour. Add the spices and extracts.

In a large bowl, stir together the baking powder and flour. With your hands, knead in 5½ cups of the flour, adding more if necessary to make a very stiff dough. Mix thoroughly until smooth. Wrap the dough tightly in plastic wrap and chill for at least 24 hours. Then mold and roll the dough into long rolls ½ inch in diameter. Again, wrap these tightly in plastic wrap and store in the refrigerator for up to a week. (I've actually kept this dough for two weeks in the fridge, using it as I needed it.)

Preheat the oven to 350° and line cookie sheets with baking parchment. Slice the rolls into ¼-inch slices ("cut in marble size," the original recipe reads) and place them 1 inch apart on the cookie sheets. Bake for 10 to 12 minutes, or until brown. Cool on racks.

Non-Sticky Rolled Cookies
Makes about 3 dozen cookies, depending on size of cookie cutters used.

My heart always leaps with joy when I see a magazine article called "Fifty Cookie Recipes from One Dough." Then my lip always curls with scorn when I actually read the article. They never mean you can make one huge batch of dough and turn it into many kinds of cookies. They always want you to make a small batch of dough and add some chocolate to it . . . and then make another small batch of dough using brown sugar instead of white . . . and then make another small batch of dough with an extra egg and some coconut . . . Well, yeah, of course you can get fifty cookie recipes if you make a new batch of dough each time! What I wanted was for them to say, "Take two cups of the BASIC DOUGH RECIPE and add . . ." When I write that magazine article, that's what it's going to say.

While you're waiting for that happy day, here's a recipe for rolled sugar cookies that *really won't stick* to the rolling pin. (Part of the reason for that is that the dough is rolled out between sheets of baking parchment, which is a little cheat-y. On the other hand, boy, is it easier. Baking parchment is just about my favorite kitchen product.) They also won't puff and spread and become unrecognizable. What's the point of using cookie cutters if the stars, angels, and donkeys all turn into clouds?

Small children (as you may have noticed) love making rolled cookies. That is, they love the concept, and they love putting sprinkles on the dough and frosting on the baked cookies. They often get bored by the actual process of rolling, cutting, rerolling the scraps, baking, waiting for the cookies to cool, and so on. That's why, when I'm baking with kids, I usually roll out the cookie dough into many shapes and have it ready on the cookie sheets for the kids to decorate. And by "decorate," I mean "pour sprinkles all over the kitchen floor." Christmas cookies come but once a year, thank God.

2½ cups unbleached flour

¾ cup sugar

¼ teaspoon salt

1 cup (2 sticks) unsalted butter, at room temperature

2 teaspoons vanilla extract

2 tablespoons cream cheese, at room temperature

With an electric mixer, beat the flour, sugar, and salt for 30 seconds. Turn the mixer to low and add the butter, one tablespoon at a time. Mix for at least 1 minute, until the dough is crumbly and dampish. Beat in the vanilla and cream cheese until the dough begins to clump together. Knead it with your hands until it's smooth and, well, doughy.

Divide the dough into 2 equal portions and pat each portion into a disk about ½ inch thick. Wrap each disk in plastic wrap and chill for at least 30 minutes and up to 3 days. (You can also freeze the dough for up to 3 weeks. Thaw it in the refrigerator before you use it.)

Set oven rack in the middle of the oven and preheat to 375°. Working with one dough disk at a time and keeping the other chilled, roll out the dough between two sheets of baking parchment to a thickness of ⅛ inch. Slide the sheets of parchment onto a cookie sheet and chill the sheet for 10 minutes while you repeat the procedure with the other dough disk.

While the second sheet of dough is chilling, cut out shapes from the first sheet. (This is one dough whose scraps can easily be gathered up and rerolled after being chilled.) Put them 2 inches apart on—yes!—a baking sheet lined with yet more baking parchment. Decorate as desired with sprinkles, red hots, and those tooth-shattering silver dragees. Repeat with the rest of the dough. Aren't you getting sick of this? That's why it's so good to get the rolling part of the process out of the way before you call in the kids.

Bake the cookies for 10 minutes, or until golden brown. Cool on a rack.

Conclusion

Tiptoeing Away from Christmas

(instead of kicking it under the carpet)

Twelfth Night was over; the decorations were down; Christmas (which, like all extremes, dates easily) seemed as *démodé* as a hat in a passport photograph: and still Mrs. Miniver had not bought herself a new engagement book, but was scribbling untidy notes on the fly-leaf of the old one.

—JAN STROTHER, *MRS. MINIVER*

"I'm sorry, Christmas, but we're terminating you."

I can never believe how many people throw out their Christmas tree on January 1. It's so brutal! The twelve days of Christmas are only half over. Why start the New Year on such a gloomy note? Don't you have enough leftover New Year's Eve depression anyway?

It's a regional thing, I know. Where I live, in Connecticut, many people leave their trees up and lit until at least mid-January; I know one family that keeps theirs up until March 1. Christmas lights on houses around here often don't come down until after Valentine's Day. Maybe it's because the nights here are so long and cold that we can't bear to return to unlit darkness. In any case, the end of Christmas isn't nearly so sad if it's allowed to fade away gradually. Leave the decorations up for as long as they still feel festive. When they start to look an-

Whisper What You'll Bring to Me—Tell Me If You Can!

Each year my sister in Atlanta sends us unusual, interesting Christmas gifts, often with a southern motif. One year, we opened her gift to discover a large (about eighteen inches high) rectangular block of wood shaped like an obelisk with several dozen long aluminum nails sticking out of it. After trying without success to think what this might be, my husband and I concluded that, as we had several remodeling jobs going on, we could use the nice aluminum nails and the block of wood would be a great firestarter for our fireplace. Only later did we find out what our mysterious gift was. My sister called to tell us she had sent a Williamsburg Apple Tree for our dining room table. We, of course, were to provide the apples.—S. M.

noying and outdated—a moment I promise that you'll recognize—*then* they can come down.

Whenever you do it, de-Christmasizing your house is a melancholy task. One year, my friend Denise decided to see if she could turn it into a new family tradition. She made a fire, put out plates of cookies, turned on soft Christmas music, and hoped that her family would rally 'round to help her. I think you can guess what happened next.

Face it, you're likely to be on your own—unless you can bear to *force* your family to help you, which I never can. I'm supposed to be a grown-up, after all; the end of Christmas is sad enough for me, but it's a tragedy for children who have to go back to school after a long vacation.

Post-Christmas you are truly The Little Red Christmas Hen—and there's nothing to do but dig in. Still, you can pace yourself. Do the job by increments. Put all the tree ornaments on trays one day; put them into their boxes the next. Have a glass of wine or sneak bites of some kind of treat as you work. The Little Red Christmas Hen has to grab what comfort is available to her.

Speaking of treats: I used to find that on the last day of the children's vacation, when we were all pitched in gloom, I would eat an unbelievable amount of leftover Christmas food. Really cram it in. Slice after slice of cold plum pudding; stale cookies; neglected candy I found when I was putting the stockings away. My stomach would actually *hurt* by bedtime.

Sometimes I was eating food I didn't even care about. One year, as I glumly forked up some cold creamed onions, it suddenly occurred to me what was going on, and I gave myself a little talk. "I know you're imagining you can keep Christmas inside you by eating all this stuff," I said to myself. "Well, you can't. But go ahead and keep eating if it makes you feel better. Maybe in a few years you'll realize that a stomach full of old Christmas leftovers isn't worth it."

And that was—very gradually—what happened. I have no problem with eating to cheer myself up as long as I know that's what I'm doing. On the other hand, I do know that if I keep cramming in leftovers, I'll end up feeling even less happy than when I started. I try to stash away a few really good Christmas treats to have after the holidays so that at least I won't be treating myself as a garbage disposal.

The terrible thank-yous

The Christmas Eve that Laura was six and a half, David was tucking her into bed when she suddenly sat up in horror. "Oh, no!" she gasped. "Thank-you notes!"

I know just what she meant.

I'm still dreading the thank-you notes I didn't write people three years ago, let alone the ones I didn't do this past Christmas. The longer I put it off, the better I imagine a note is going to have to be when I finally do write it—and with some of the notes I owe at this point, I'd have to write in liquid platinum to make them worthy of their lateness. Even worse is the fact that

I owe several condolence notes as well. And as for the wedding presents I still haven't given people—!

It's too late for me: I've permanently absorbed the idea that thank-you notes are a deadly form of obligation instead of a fun way of making other people happy. But it may not be too late for your children. If you're lucky, you get them young enough that they still care about pleasing people. "Let's show Pop-Pop how much you liked the truck! He'll be so happy to know!" That kind of thing. For this to work, you need to start out when the child should probably be so little that he or she still can't write at all; you have him draw a picture and dictate what to say. If several presents need to be mentioned, making a collage with magazine cutouts works well, too.

As the child gets older, you can help her understand that thank-you notes can actually be fun to write. When I was a child, mine were so dull and formulaic that it's no wonder I hated writing them. If I got stationery, for example, I invariably used a piece of it for my thank-you note and wrote, "As you can see, I'm using it now!" I always wrote the bulk of the letter about the present and then added one or two sentences about my life before signing off. In fourth grade, I wrote that my sister and I were taking swimming lessons. "I dive, and Cathy jumps. Love, Ann," I wrote. In eighth grade, I finished a note to my grandparents with, "Everything's fine here, except that I'm tired all the time." They called my parents to make sure I wasn't sick.

What I didn't understand then was that a thank-you note is supposed to have a very short thank-you section and a longer here's-the-news section—and that the news section can be funny. The funnier the letter is, the shorter it can be.

My children, fortunately, understood this early, and they always get their notes mailed (relatively) on time. Here's a note Laura wrote to my sister and brother-in-law when she was six:

Dear Cathy and Mark
Thank you for my colored pencils. I love them. My faverite is ma-
genta. The other day Shortie [the dog] spent two hours eating

garbage. She also ate some of my candy making supplies. She is as
fat as a bag of water, and she has to stay in the bathroom. She sits
near the heater. Love, Laura.

Last Christmas, my parents gave John a sweater for Christmas and a check for his birthday, which is on January 5. He wrote them that he liked the sweater so much that he had used the birthday check to buy another sweater just like it.

And once, when David got his precious, precious electric drill for Christmas, he drilled several holes through his thank-you note to demonstrate the drill's efficacy.

I wish I could go into more depth on this topic, but I have a lot of thank-you notes to write.

The rest of the year

Speaking of Christmas, which I hope is what we've been doing all this time: To a great extent, many of the ideas I've suggested in this book work for other holidays, too.

In particular, we should all stop defining holidays by their calendar dates. I'm not saying you should play April Fool's Day tricks on May 10 or take your kids trick-or-treating on November 3. But you should adjust your calendar to suit the holiday—not the other way around. Remember, *dates don't matter*.

Thanksgiving is a prime example of a holiday that falls at a bad time. Most kids don't get out of school until Wednesday; most adults get Friday off as well as Thursday. Why not move your Thanksgiving dinner to Friday or even Saturday or Sunday? That way, the family doesn't have to plunge into ferocious cooking the second everyone gets home on Wednesday night.

If you suddenly realize you need an ingredient on Friday or Saturday, you can easily find a supermarket that's open. (I'll leave it to you to explain to the checkout clerk why you're buying canned pumpkin and cranberries the day after Thanksgiving.) You also have the chance to invite a broader range of guests, since most of your friends and family will already have celebrated their Thanksgiving and will be free to come to yours. (I'll leave it to your guests to decide if they feel like having fresh turkey and stuffing when that's what they've been eating for the past several meals.) In households where football is an important part of Thanksgiving, family members can concentrate on the game on Thursday and on the meal the day after that, instead of infuriating the cook by grabbing their plates and vanishing into the den for the rest of the day.

Moving the celebration to a convenient day also works for birthdays and anniversaries, as long as the celebrants are mature enough.

The January blues

No matter how tired of Christmas you may be by its end, it's still a blow to have it over. Christmas feels like a pregnancy that way. You waited and waited. Now the baby's born and you're exhausted, and you've lost that festive sense of anticipation to tide you over.

Here it can be helpful to ask yourself why you're sad and what you feel as though you're missing. What were you hoping Christmas would accomplish that it hasn't accomplished? Why do you feel as though you flunked?

You may find that part of the answer has to do with magic. No matter how old we get, we still expect Christmas to do more for us than it possibly can. Even if we don't let ourselves get tired; even if we stretch the holiday out to its full twelve days and more; even if we train ourselves to stop being micromanaging Christmas Coordinators and become effective Christmas Delegators . . . even so, we'll probably never outgrow the idea that Christmas *can* be perfect. That the Christmas spirit *can* light up our hearts and keep them lit for as long as we want. That if we only look hard enough, we might catch a glimpse of Santa.

Not much to do about wishing things were magic, is there?

Our Family's Worst Christmas Songs

1. "Blue Christmas," sung by Elvis. We have to turn this off before Elvis goes "Ooo-ooo-ooo-oo" or my daughter Dale goes ballistic.

2. "Christmas Shoes" by Newsong. This is manipulative *and* implausible. "Sir, I want to buy these shoes for my Mama, please/ It's Christmas Eve and these shoes are just her size." What boy knows his mom's shoe size? And wouldn't the sales clerk *know* it's Christmas Eve?

3. "Grandma Got Run Over By a Reindeer." So stupid.

4. "The Holiday Season," aka "Happy Holiday." We hate the lines "He'll be coming down the chimney down" and "Whoop de doo and hickory dock, and don't forget to hang up your sock."

5. "I'll Be Home for Christmas." This is really a great song— except for the line "Please have snow and mistletoe, and presents *on* the tree," which makes us all nuts.

6. We just hate when "My Favorite Things" is a Christmas song because it has warm woolen mittens and snowflakes that stay on your nose and eyelashes.

7. All of us, but especially my son Doug, abhor "The Little Drummer Boy." Who would play drums for a newborn baby?—C. K.

But some of the reasons you're sad may be grounded in the real world. Maybe you wish you'd spent more time with the children, or performed a charitable act for someone who needed it more than your family. You might wish you could become closer to a relative—or simply stop asking so much of yourself on festive occasions.

If you identify some of your post-Christmas feelings this way, you're lucky. Because fortunately (and unfortunately), the real gifts Christmas is supposed to bring us are always around, waiting for us to reach out toward them. Real-world frustrations can be worked on in real time. You don't need to wait until next Christmas to try again.

Can you believe this book is almost done and I haven't quoted from *A Christmas Carol* once? Not only is a Dickens quote required by law in all Christmas books, but Dickens is my favorite, favorite author. In addition to being a great writer, Dickens had a pet raven named Grip, and I've always *wanted* a pet raven!

Every Christmas I used to try to read *A Christmas Carol* aloud to the kids until they finally tired of my wrenching sobs every time Tiny Tim died, and decreed that they would read it for themselves if they felt like it. So far, neither of them has felt like it. I guess I wrecked it for them. More Christmas guilt . . .

I still can't resist ending this book with an appropriate passage from *A Christmas Carol*, though. Let's see. There are so many good ones. It can't be "God bless us every one"—that's way too obvious.

"Awakening in the middle of a prodigiously tough snore . . ." I guess that's not quite right.

"Business! . . . Mankind was my business. The common welfare was my business; charity, mercy, forbearance, and benevolence were, all, my business." Getting closer, but . . .

No, no, no, here it is:

"I will honour Christmas in my heart, and try to keep it all the year. I will live in the Past, the Present, and the Future. The Spirits of all Three shall strive within me. I will not shut out the lessons that they teach."

There.

Index